Reflections from
a Restless Mind

Reflections from a Restless Mind

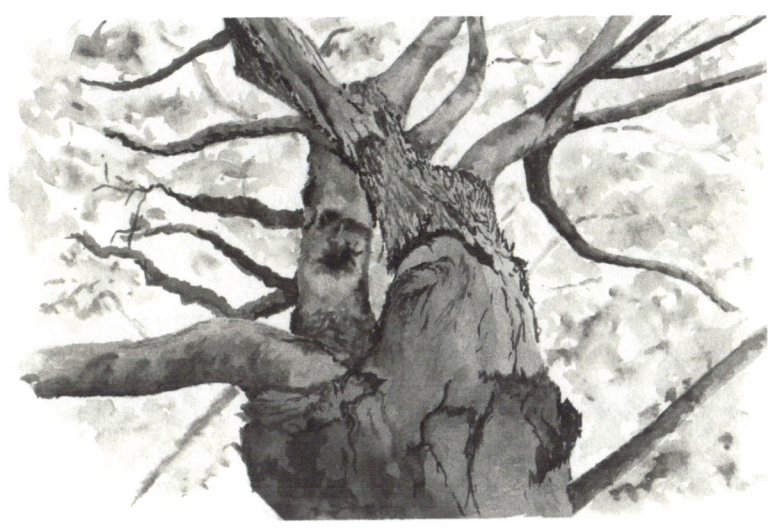

Dorothy Canote

Compass Flower Press
Columbia, Missouri

Published by Compass Flower Press
Columbia, MO 65203

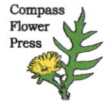
Compass
Flower
Press

Library of Congress Control Number: 2020916895
ISBN: 978-1-951960-07-0

Cover painting: The shagbark hickory, among the hardest and hardiest of our native trees, typifies the qualities of my fellow native Missourians—rugged, full of character, and most at home in the woods and countrysides of Missouri.

We do not need magic to transform our world.
We carry all of the power we need inside ourselves already.

—J.K. Rowling

'Late people do not altogether leave us,' she thought, 'they are still with us in our memories, such that, wherever we are, no matter what time of the day it is or how we were feeling, they are there, still shining the light of their love upon us.'

—Alexander McCall Smith,
The Woman Who Walked in Sunshine

Dedication

This book is dedicated to the women in my family, all of whom learned to rely on themselves and who taught me, by example, how to rely on myself.

My mother, Mary Frances (Fullerton) Deardorff, who allowed me to explore and whose love and guidance taught me respect for a great many things.

My maternal grandmother, Jesse (Dunlap) Fullerton, who cared for me in my childhood and who bequeathed me her memories.

My maternal great-grandmother, Margaret (Parkinson) Dunlap, who brought with her across the ocean her genes, a part of which are mine.

And finally, my smart and talented daughters, Angela Elizabeth England and Jennifer Roxanne (England) Townsend who, although they are as different as night and day, can sing a beautiful song together.

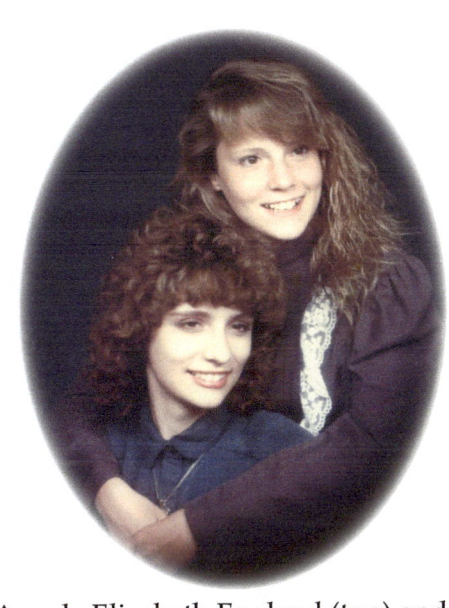

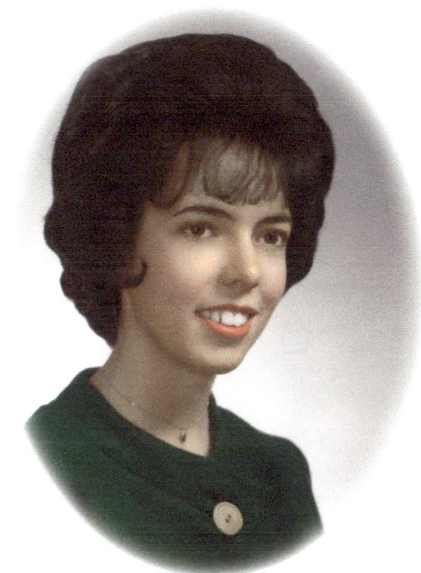

Dorothy (Deardorff) (England) Canote

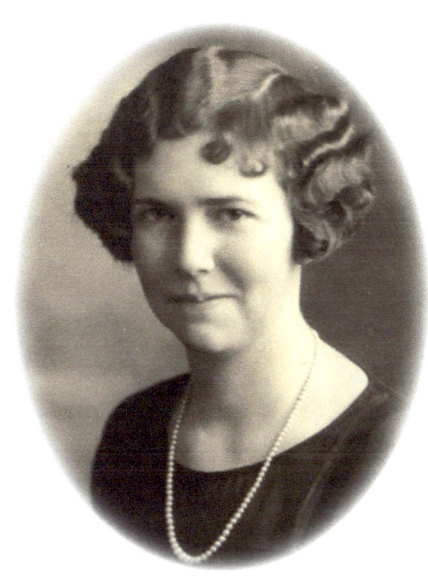

Angela Elizabeth England (top) and
Jennifer Roxanne (England) Townsend

Mary Frances (Fullerton) Deardorff

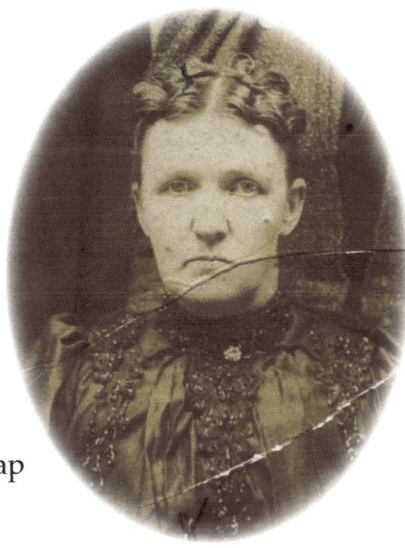

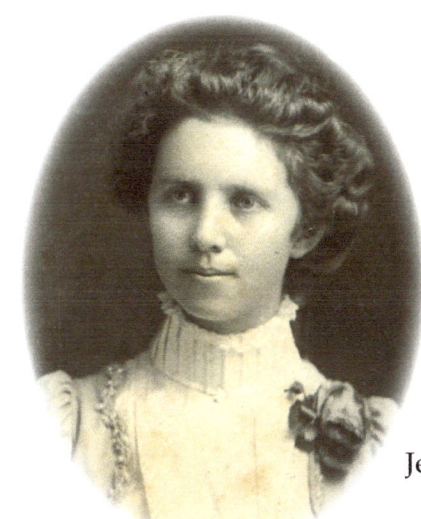

Margaret (Parkinson) Dunlap

Jesse (Dunlap) Fullerton

Foreword

The Power of Knowing Who We Are

The dedication for this book deserves more than a few lines. When I started thinking about to whom I owed the greatest love and satisfaction for my life, all my thoughts went immediately to the women in my life—my mother, followed closely by my maternal grandmother, and then of course, my daughters.

In the past dozen years I have been pursuing my family tree, an interest many in our society have taken up following the recent advances in DNA analysis and availability of inexpensive genetic testing. During a summer course for teachers offered through the University of Missouri's biochemistry department, a blood sample revealed some information about my maternal lineage that opened a window on my thinking. This information was encoded in mitochondrial DNA.

Mitochondrial DNA

And here comes the teacher again. If you are bored by biology you can just skip this section, but if you read it you will have a better understanding of how this ancestry works.

The significance of mitochondrial DNA is tied into the process by which cells and their interior organelles evolved. Both mitochondria and plant chloroplasts are tiny structures found within cells, believed to be derived from invading bacteria. Chloroplasts are descendants of early photosynthetic (autotrophic) bacteria capable of manufacturing sugars from carbon dioxide and water, while mitochondria, descended from nonphotosynthetic (heterotrophic) bacteria, are tiny factories that use the energy stored in the bonds of sugar to create heat and to do the chemical work within the cell.

From evidence in prehistoric fossil remains, it is reasonably thought that these bacteria invaded cells and thrived there in a mutually beneficial (symbiotic) relationship, a means of protection from the harsh conditions of early Earth. Both organelles have their own DNA, not in the filamentous chromosomes one usually sees depicted in media, but as a circular structure which is capable of replicating to produce more of each organelle.

Moving on to sex (always a topic of interest), when cells differentiated into different types and moved from simple single-cell reproduction to dimorphic sex cells (sperm and egg) the difference in their structures was significant. The sperm cell is basically a delivery system for DNA, very small, with a tail for swimming and a single-copy package of DNA from the male parent. The egg, on the other hand, is a proportionately larger cell holding the corresponding set of chromosomes from the female parent as well as all the organelles needed for cell function. These include quantities of mitochondria sufficient for a fertilized egg to mature and divide and to eventually form the multicellular organism—in this case, us.

As a result of this process, virtually all the mitochondrial DNA comes from the female egg cell and is thus passed from the maternal ancestor to offspring. With sperm-producing sons there is little or no mitochondrial DNA passed on, so that only the females of a family line continue that inheritance.

Who Am I?

Analysis of my mitochondrial DNA revealed what is called Icelandic (northern European) ancestry, which fits with what I have been able to find out about where my people came from.

Counting my mother as generation one, I can follow my maternal linage back five generations to Scotland in 1871. It was not too hard to go further back on my grandfather's side, but the custom of the wife assuming the husband's family name makes it easy to lose the path to female ancestors. Regardless of nit-picky details, the linage on my maternal grandfather's side goes back seven generations to the sister of a Scottish queen.

So who cares? Only we family history addicts who love a good mystery. But it was only when I began to think of the influence of historical events on immigration that I began to understand where and who I came from. And regardless of their importance to the rest of the world, to me it has been empowering.

Table of Contents

Preface

What a trip! I never dreamed when I started writing for my first book, *Paintings and Musings from the Heartland,* that the book would be so warmly received by so many readers. My editor and I were ready to do a book launch and signing in the spring of 2020 when events collided—or as one might say, the poop hit the fan. Just about the time the COVID-19 outbreak started, I developed a mitral valve malfunction that necessitated open heart surgery just as the nation, the state, and all normal domestic activity shut down.

Nevertheless, having forewarned all friends and family on my Christmas card list, I had modest success in otherwise unpublicized sales. I was enthusiastically supported by my fellow artists as well as a number of family members and old friends, and word of mouth was responsible for a trickle of outgoing mailings. So as my friend Gladys said when I told her I was starting on a second book, "You've been bitten by the bug, haven't you?" Not exactly a question because we both knew that yes, I had.

My hometown of Avalon, Missouri and the stories shared of the history of that area generated the most interest by far. I had a number of long phone conversations with long-time Livingston County residents and their kin, as well as expatriates like myself who had moved away but not forgotten their childhood and experiences there.

I hadn't exhausted my collection of photos and possibilities for painting subjects, so I decided to try to dredge up some more information and create more paintings and stories to go with them. As with all my essays and paintings, these are also in some way a part of my life and experiences.

The Middle Years

In the writings I have chosen to share with my readers, you may note the absence of certain periods of my life, namely what I will refer to as the early middle years. Those were the years during which I was fully engaged with marriage and a teaching career, and having my two daughters, Angela and Jennifer. I started graduate school during those years, and then became divorced. I can only blame a case of middle-age crazies for that period of time. While the divorce was in no way as bad as some, it was still painful for everyone involved. My ex-husband David and I are still friends and keep in touch. His wife Susan is also a dear friend and I think of her as the sister I never had. It was only after I started grad school that fresh new episodes of a more adventurous part of my life unfolded.

This Book

Chapter One, "Back to Avalon," is devoted to more of the little town's infrastructure and include my own and others' memories of its buildings and people. If there are errors in those stories, I hope my readers will contact me and let me know.

Chapter Two is a miscellany of paintings and topics inspired by current events and totally erratic sources. Not much else to say about that.

Trying to settle on something that might make interesting reading, I decided to relate some life experiences and adventures of what I call my later middle years.

Chapter Three, "Walks on the Wild Side," may not seem too wild to some of my more adventurous readers but for a simple country girl from a conservative Republican family they are practically heretical. Now I have a leaning toward the Democrats, with a good dose of irreverent Independents thrown in. I also shared some interesting stories about my caving friends and our adventures below ground.

Chapter Four, "Mexico: To the Border and Beyond," is about some of my southbound trips, to the Rio Grande and into Mexico.

You will possibly note that, compared to my first literary effort, I am considerably more verbose. I chose this time around to select the essay topics first and then do the paintings. It turned out I have more to say than I expected. I hope you will consider it worth the effort to read.

It was the sort of paradise that people move through
unconsciously before they understand that what you love
can whiffle away like a dandelion bloom, beyond your
reach in the length of a breath.

—Carrie La Seur, *The Home Place*

Chapter One
Back to Avalon

If some of the references in these stories seem obscure, I will refer you to my previous book, Paintings and Musings from the Heartland, which devotes one whole chapter to Avalon and its history, layout, and some of its people and buildings. Otherwise I prefer not to regress.

Many of the paintings in this book were done from old black and white photographs from my mother's albums. Many had people in the photos, but as my people-painting skills in my opinion leave something to be desired, people were left out.

Also, for those of you who knew, lived, and grew up in Avalon, keep in mind that some of what you read may be incomplete or not what you recall. These are my memories and the facts as I have been able to verify them from certain old Avalonians. This writing and painting is an adventure for me like the stories were. It sure beats waiting around for a stinking virus to go away.

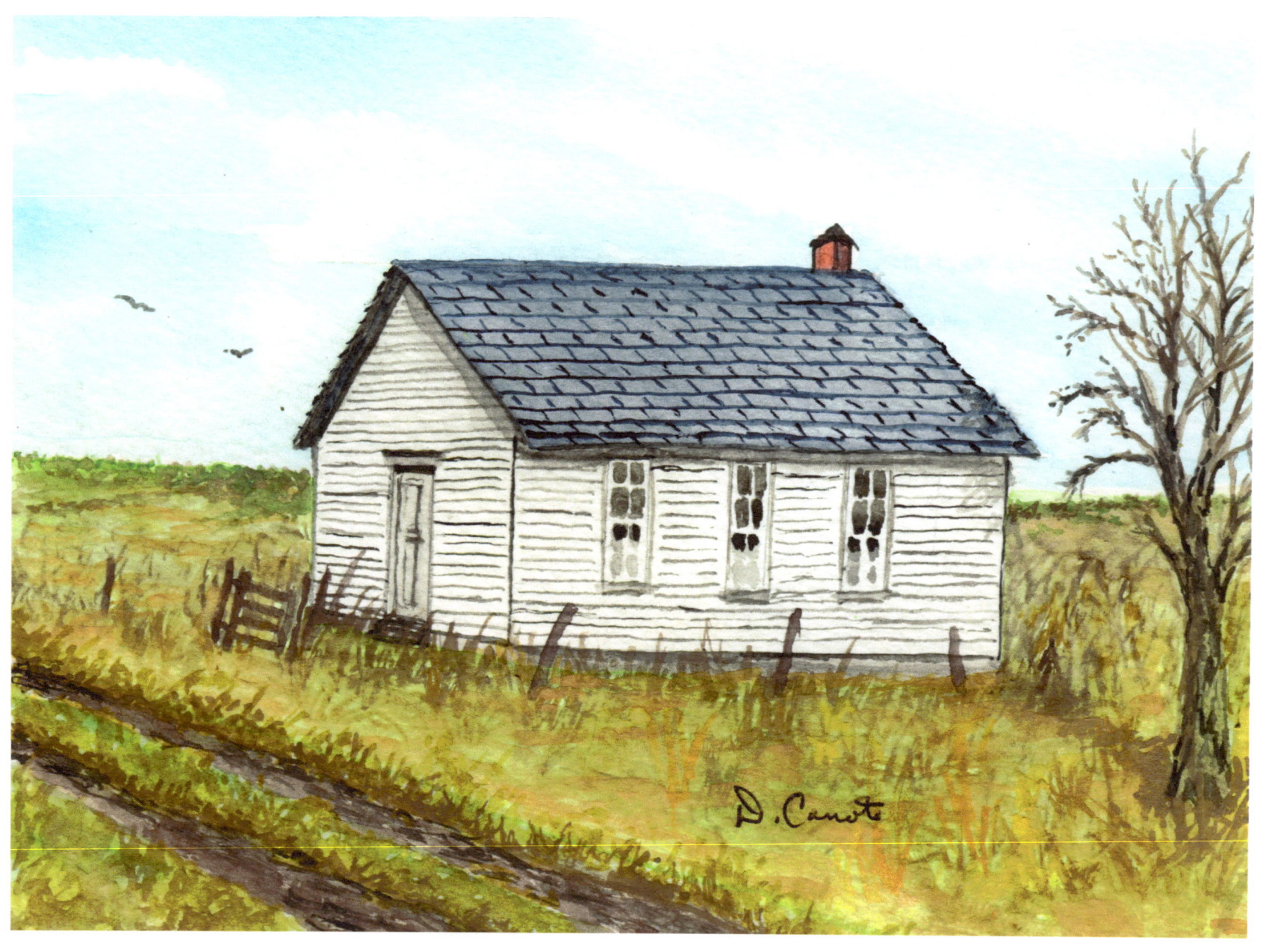

Lowland School

Sitting alone in the midst of northern Missouri prairie, this little one-room school was where my mother held her first job. She attended Northwest Missouri State Teacher's College (now NWMSU) for a one-year program to earn her teaching certificate. She held the job only until she married my father, because at that time married women were evidently not deemed to be suitable role models for young minds.

Located two miles north and a quarter-mile west of Avalon on what is now Route JJ, the school was the norm for years before the era of good paved roads. While most small towns had village schools, commuting was mostly on foot or horseback and it was not convenient for rural children to travel perhaps five miles (one way) or more each day. Even today, as you travel the country byroads of Missouri and other states it is not uncommon to see these small buildings still standing, some used for storing hay, some perhaps remodeled into simple homes, but most are simply in disrepair and falling into the landscape. And of course many are already gone.

The ephemeral nature of human infrastructure has really been brought home to me as I researched and reflected on the changes that have occurred during my own lifetime. As a baby boomer, I began on the cusp of many societal and environmental changes: improvements in medicine, agriculture, and transportation, enhanced educational practices, economic and workplace equality for women, and a better understanding and appreciation for the impact of human-produced changes in the natural environment.

During the twenty-two years I spent teaching in Missouri classrooms, I often had occasion to think back to my own experience when I was going to school. Avalon's six elementary grades were split into two classrooms, one teacher for each, and I greatly admire the men and women who endured the low pay and often poor conditions to train and sometimes even inspire young minds to become functioning members of society. Following the example of those teachers, during the time that I taught, I tried to always remember that each student came into the classroom with a different level of ability and socioeconomic background, as well as his or her own set of problems, feelings, and expectations—or lack thereof.

I expect many parents at the time I write this are gaining a better appreciation of what it is to be a home schooling teacher because of COVID-19 virus and schooling changes. They only have to put up with their own children, which they can discipline if necessary (and hopefully lovingly) without fear of supervisory oversight. At the same time they are free to pat, hug, and otherwise show physical affection without being accused of unworthy motives.

I loved my years of teaching, in spite of the daily frustrations and challenges. As any worthy teacher will tell you, they put up with the weeks or even months of frustration and headaches for the reward of that one day when a student's eyes light up with understanding and the spark of meaningful learning is lit in their mind. Teaching is then not a job, it is a reward.

My Grandmother Jesse's House

My grandmother Jesse, with whom I stayed a lot as a child, lived in a small one-story house on the far east end of Avalon. My Grandpa Van was a carpenter and built the house which they lived in their entire married life. They raised their children, Helen, Maude, Mary Frances, Pauline and James, in that house, and there Grandpa died in 1950. Perhaps it would be more proper to say it was my grandparents' house, but I barely recall my Grandpa Van in it, as I was only four years old when he passed away.

Water was acquired using a hand pump from a cistern located under the cement-covered front porch, and it was normal to keep an enamel bucket of water and a long-handled dipper on a table by the kitchen door. In northern parts of Missouri, the soil is heavily mineralized as a result of ice-age glaciation, and the ground water has a distinctive flavor that is still on my memory's tongue. Add to that the taste imparted by drinking from a tin cup and you have all you need to be that person, back in that place at that time.

Also on the porch was the ubiquitous wooden swing suspended from the ceiling. It provided a lovely place to sit on summer evenings or, padded by a quilt, a lovely place for grandkids to nap on hot summer afternoons.

In the back yard to the east was a huge old pear tree that had the most delicious pears you could imagine. The front and west yards were shaded by sap-oozing elm trees that dropped twigs and small limbs on a regular basis. Grandma had the old type of two-wheel horizontal rotary blade mower that was jammed up by these twigs, so it was the job of whichever grandchild was staying with her at the time to do pick-up duty before the grass was mowed.

And it had to be mowed often to keep the grass short enough to spot snakes. The black rat snake, aka black snake, can grow to a considerable size, around six feet long, and was a feared predator on eggs and baby chicks in the hen house. Grandma hated those snakes and kept her trusty hoe nearby all summer. The lawn was beautiful when mown, consisting entirely of the bluegrass prevalent throughout that part of the country before the introduction of the darned tall fescue.

A smoke house and root cellar were located behind the house. The chicken house and attached outhouse were farther away at the back of the lot, accessed through a fenced chicken yard. There was also a garage, its use originally to house Grandpa Fullerton's old Model T Ford, long gone in my days, as was Grandpa. At the time I was there it was (as garages tend to be) full of tools, machine parts, and a miscellany of potentially useful items too valuable to throw away. One of these items was a hand-cranked corn grinder, used to grind corn for the chickens. That scent of ground corn as well as that from oil, soil, and all the other farmy smells is another of my residual memories. Also stored there, safely away from the house, was a big metal drum of kerosene, known in those days as coal oil, not in use so much these days, but essential at that time.

There was a barn to the west across a small section of pasture that at one time kept a milk cow in graze. When I was near school age, Grandma also took care of my still-close and much beloved cousin Leroy. He was about ten years old and the oldest of Uncle Jim's offspring. This was at about the time of the Korean War, and evidently Leroy had a developed a fascination with the idea of planes and radios and spotters and so forth, and had set up a

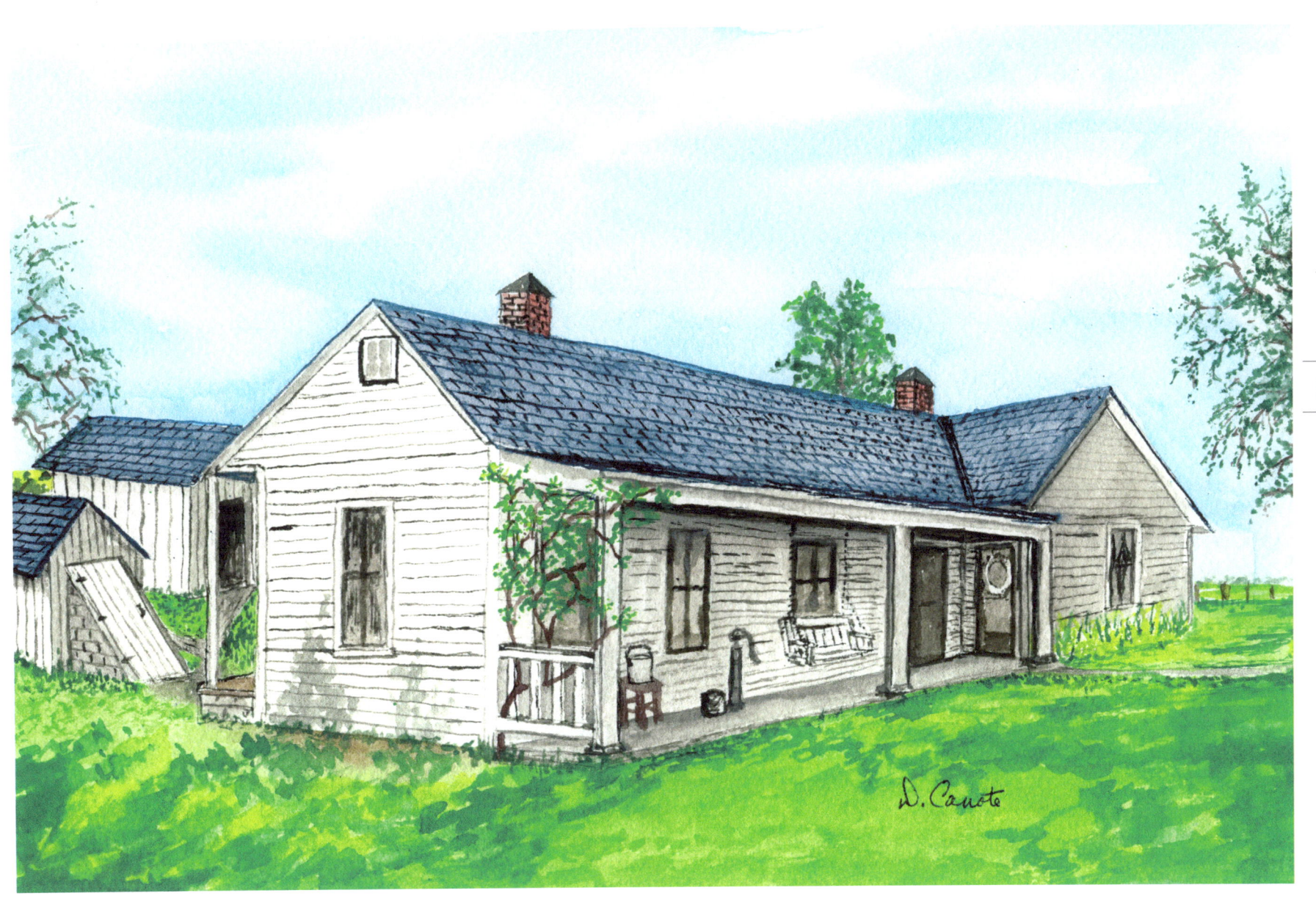

wood box replica of a radio receiver in a small room in the front of the barn. Being about four years old and curious, I braved the trip from the yard to the barn to see what he was doing.

Well, Leroy wasn't having any of it and sort of barked at me to "Go away!" He was also pretty possessive of a cool red metal toy Jeep, about the size of a shoe box and with a horn that would go *OOK* when you pressed the steering wheel. I never got to play with that either. He really wasn't very good at sharing, but I have forgiven him.

Inside the house I recall a quite a few of the furnishings in the rooms, especially the kitchen area. Early on in my stays with Grandma she still had one of those big old wood- or coal-fired ranges in the kitchen, with the water reservoir on the side. She had one of the early ice boxes, so called because they kept the cold by placing a big block of ice in a lower section. The rest was lead- or zinc-lined, or sometimes porcelain, which deterred rust. A man came by on a regular schedule and brought in the ice block with a pair of wicked looking tongs. I kept a safe distance.

A back door opened out of the kitchen onto the covered back porch. When it was laundry day, hot water was hauled from the stove out to the wash tub, where the wash got stomped with a metal plunger-looking thing, then into the rinse tub and then fed through the hand crank wringer before being hauled out to the clothes line for some sunshine—hopefully.

Off the kitchen on the north side of the house, a tiny pantry, maybe six by six feet in size, made an 'ell' that increased the house's depth. With shelves on the right-hand wall, there was only enough space to walk in and take about two steps to the right. From there you could either cook on the stove or work at a table. If you looked straight in, there was also a small gap against the north wall between the cabinet and table, just big enough to slide a kitchen stool in place. It was there I watched my grandmother do much of her cooking.

She had a two-burner coal oil stove in the pantry over whose flame she sometimes toasted slices of homemade bread for my breakfast. The bread was made on the small wooden table using flour scooped out of a hopper/flour bin in the bottom of a side-board cabinet, and baked in an oven placed on top of the two-burner stove. Her bread and cinnamon rolls were the best, the rolls coming out of the oven with a hardened candy coating on the under side. Heavenly!

Walking from kitchen to the next room, which was the dining room, there was a cylindrical Warm Morning wood stove that shared a common chimney flue with the big kitchen stove. It was necessary to keep a close eye on the stove pipe damper and the revolving air flow dial on the door so it didn't get too hot. We kids thought it pretty fun to see an unattended stove heat up to cherry-red hot, but as I realized later, it only takes one house fire to make it not so funny. When it was time for a full bath, cold water was put into a galvanized washtub and brought up to lukewarm by adding hot water from a teakettle. Not very fun, especially in the winter.

Grandma kept a small cot in the dining room also, for guests or naps. There she kept her treadle Singer sewing machine, which got lots of use over the years. Store-bought clothes were becoming more common, but there was always a lot of patching, darning, and mending to be done.

A largish dining table with two to four straight chairs took up much of the space, and it was there I supervised Grandma's communications procedures. She wrote letters off and on during the day as time allowed and when a writing tablet was available, but also used her kerosene (coal oil) lantern in the evenings for writing the many postcards with which she kept in touch with all the friends and relatives who had moved away.

The east room at the front of the house was a formal living room with several over-stuffed chairs and small occasional tables, as well as a big couch that had the most unpleasant fabric I have ever encountered. I don't know what it was called, but imagine thick velvet starched to the stiffness of horse hair and there you have it. As a kid, if I tried to sit on it in shorts it would stick me and leave a rash on my legs. Come to think of it, maybe that was the point—keep the kids off and company visits short. I recall getting in trouble once for rubbing my mother's cold cream (facial cream) into the fabric hoping to improve it. You can imagine how well that went over.

This was also the room where our church's Missionary Society ladies met when it was Grandma's turn to host. I got the job of serving cookies, and when I was old enough not to spill it, cups of hot tea. They mostly prayed a lot and talked about sending stuff to Africa.

In one of my increasingly frequent phone conversations with Uncle Jim's son, Leroy, he recalled that he was staying with our grandparents at the time Grandpa was dying. All the children showed up that evening and the next morning Grandpa was gone. His body was brought back from the embalmer and lay in state in the formal living room. Lee, as he goes by now, recalls the lunch (referred to as dinner in the country) and visitation. For some reason it kind of creeped me out, the thought of having lunch with a dead person lying in the next room. Well, but it's different than in a church, right? Whatever.

And now for the rest of the house. The three north rooms were bedrooms. Grandma's was just off the dining room, the small narrow middle room was reserved for the boys (mostly Leroy), and the east room was my favorite. It had a window on both the north and east wall, so in the summer you could lay with your head near the window and watch the lightning bugs do their ever-glorious blinking, and out the north window you could see the lights from Chillicothe on the horizon, a full ten miles away, and wonder what was happening there with all those lights on.

When it was cold I slept with Grandma, probably not her favorite thing, especially when I forgot to take a trip to the outhouse before dark, and had to get up and use the chamber pot. And no, of course she didn't make me empty it!

Finally, and I saved what might be the best for last, was the attic. Just outside her bedroom was a closet space under the attic stairs where interesting things were stored, and the actual stairs were accessed through her bedroom by a *really* narrow (about two feet wide), steep (think two steps up and one step forward) staircase. The attic covered the whole of the house, with a wood floor, unfinished on the walls and ceiling. There was only one bare light bulb with a pull string to light the whole length and talk about a place for creepy crawlies....

But it had boxes and trunks of mysterious stuff—artifacts from Grandpa's membership in the Modern Woodmen of America, the Odd Fellows Lodge, old dresses, shoes—you get the idea. But you had to be careful not to put small objects too near the walls, as they would disappear into the space created by the intersection of the floor with the wall studs. Leroy remembers a story about a pistol of some sort that got dropped down one of these black holes, and for all we know it's still there. We don't know why or who did it, or why Grandpa had it, but if they ever tear the house down, Lee wants it!

The Exchange Building

This building is still standing, although in a much remodeled state from its former days. According to my best source of information, Gary Rickenbrode, the building began life as a creamery. At that time farmers who had milk cows did not usually have facilities on their farms either to store or to process milk, so would bring it to the cool of the creamery where the cream was separated from the milk and then stored until it was sold or shipped to another location. As best I recall, the building was made of hollow red tile blocks rather than bricks. I am guessing about the reason for this, and would think that the block construction would make it easier to keep the room cool and to clean up after the milk handling.

From postings on the Avalon Then and Now Facebook page, I gleaned more information on its ownership. A fellow named Roy Wright sold it to W. L. McMillen who operated a grocery and feed store there. It housed the post office and home of postmaster David Hord until he constructed a new post office building in 1950.

When I was growing up the building belonged to a fellow named Forty May. I presume Forty was his nickname. There was probably some entertaining story about why he was called that. When I lived in Avalon, Forty used the building as a feed store, selling bags of grain and pre-mixed livestock feed. To walk in the store was to inhale the somewhat yeasty smell of oats and corn, as well as the sweet molasses in the prepared feeds.

Regardless of its use at the time, it was locally known as the exchange building. You might well ask where it got that name. Since there are very few people left who might know, I am going to speculate. In the prehistory of small towns, not all families had ready money to buy store-bought necessities such as flour, sugar, garden seeds, and the like. However, many town and country residents had a few chickens, home gardens, fruit trees and smoke houses for curing home-grown meats. Also, women might make hand-sewn sundries like embroidered tea towels, aprons, shirts, knit socks, and other useful items. All of these could be bartered for grocery staples or other necessities. Thus, the exchange store.

As time passed, Avalon's population declined when people moved to larger towns and cities with more and better opportunities for jobs and education. One by one the local businesses closed, with only enough remaining to service the remaining residents. The exchange building stood empty for several years, until my brother and his wife decided to open a small grocery and dry goods business there. Don and Della didn't make much money at it but it occupied their time for a bit.

Today, the building has been remodeled into a small restaurant and bar, The Playhouse, which serves some very tasty burgers, steaks, and other home-style country food. It is a popular hang-out for the locals as well as a destination for both planned and spontaneous events. The large back room is used for our annual Avalon reunion on Memorial Day weekend. It is the custom for the above-ground folks to visit the below-ground folks at the Avalon Cemetery, decorate the graves with flowers, and walk around checking on who has checked out. Then we meet in the back room of The Playhouse and 'exchange' memories and gossip about the Good Old Days.

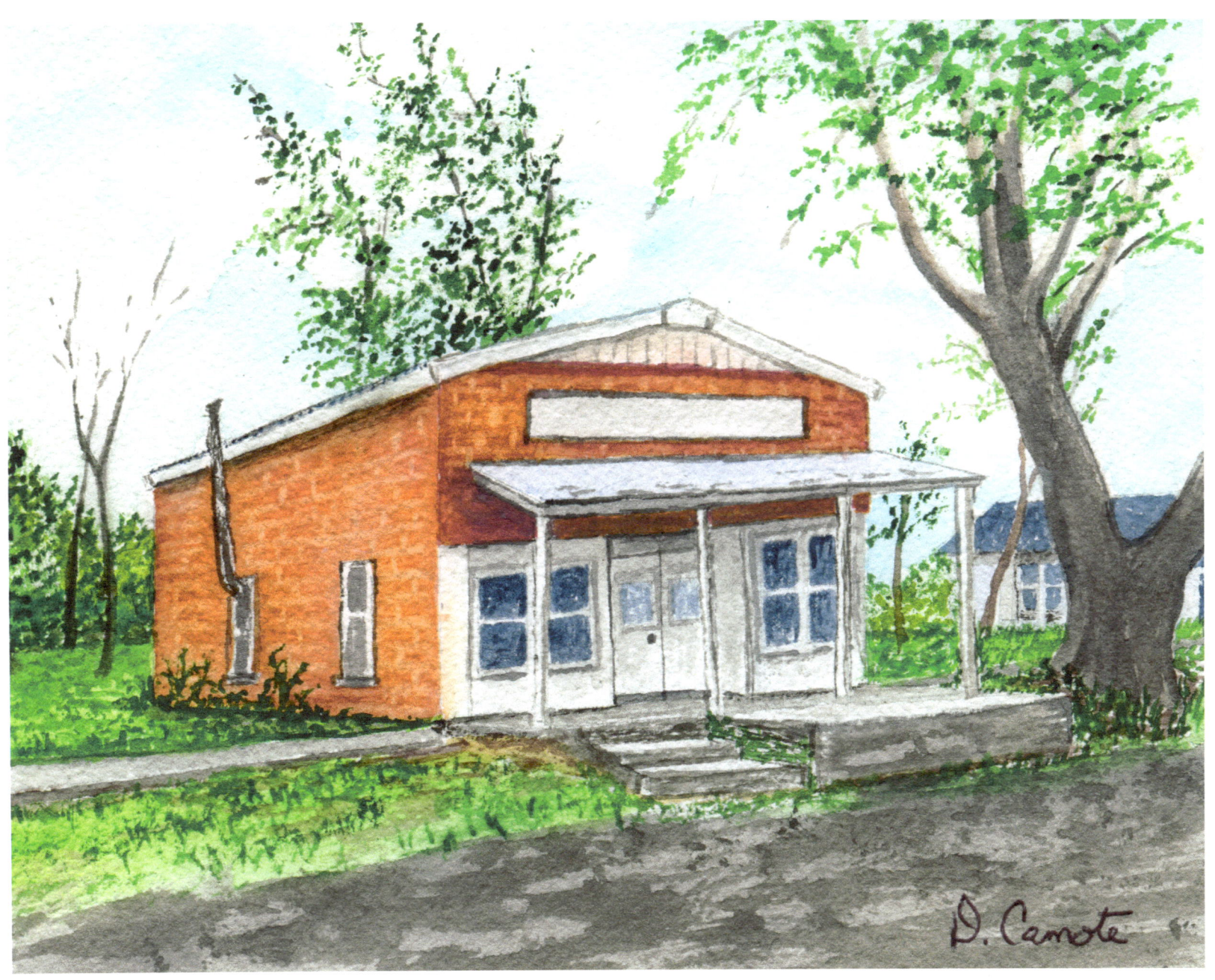

9

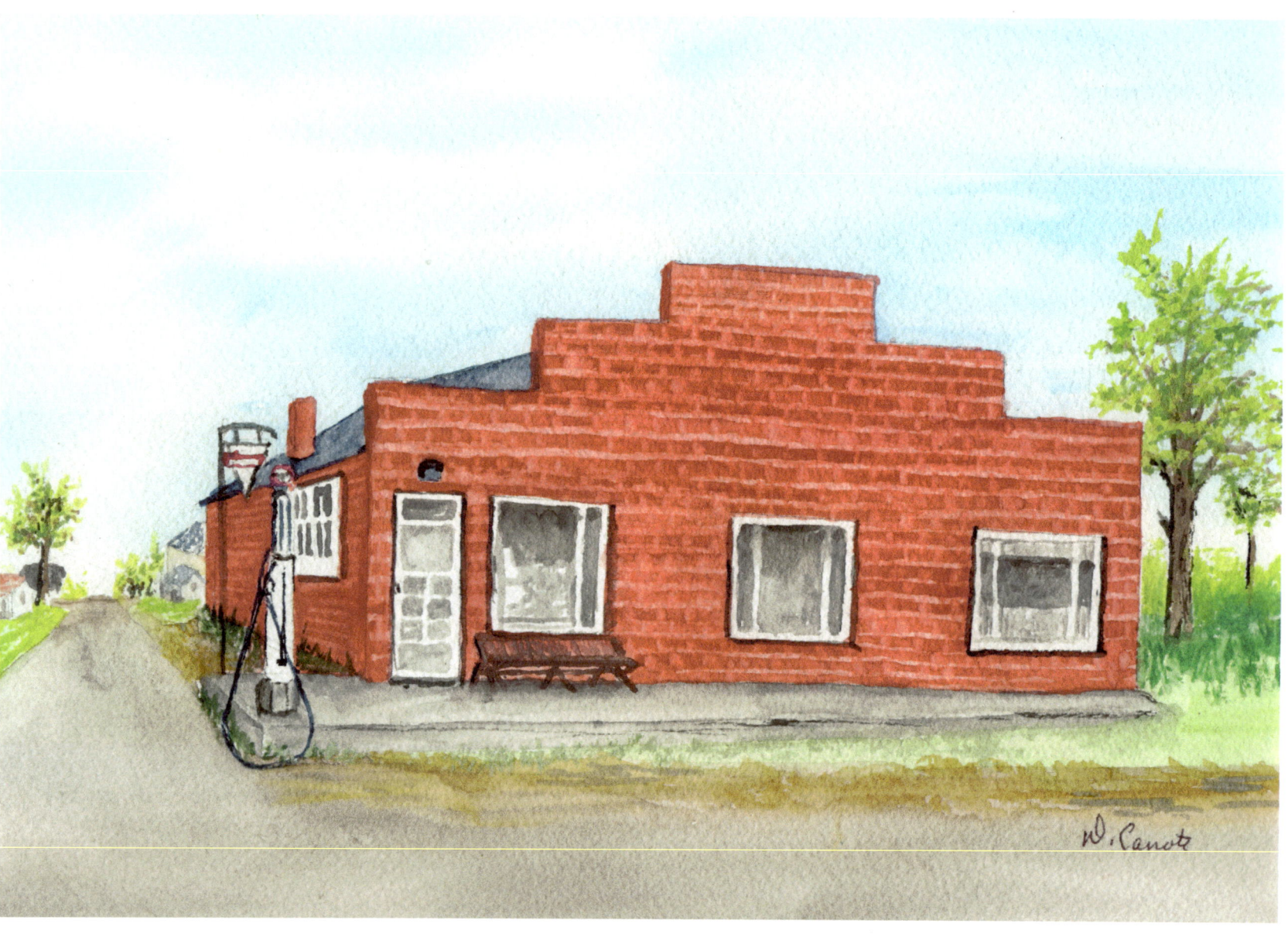

Avery's Store

This store was located on the blacktop Route H at its intersection with Route JJ, which leads north, curves west, and eventually intersects with Highway 65 leading to Chillicothe. Route JJ ends in Avalon at the intersection where the store sat, but the road continues south on gravel, leading to the Avalon Cemetery. This intersection and the Main Street intersection immediately west were probably the two most interesting locations to the old codgers and younger loafers who sat around watching Avalon's goings on. That sounds awkward, but that's how everyone referred to the daily events.

Harry Avery, his wife Bernice and children Patricia (Pat), Harry Jr. (Junior), and Gerald lived on the north end of Main Street. I spent an hour or two on the phone with Pat picking her brain for information and her memories of her dad's store, and we ended up doing a memory-based virtual tour of Avalon and its citizens. Maybe some of that will be useful later, but for now it was, wow, just a blast from the past!

Harry Avery was a man of many talents and parts. Besides the store, he was an auctioneer and also operated a trucking business, hauling livestock to the Kansas City and possibly Saint Joseph stockyards. His store was a one-story red-block building. In front was a single gasoline pump. He may have sold kerosene too, since quite a few folks didn't have electricity at that time and either went to bed with the chickens or used a kerosene lantern for after-dark activities. He also was in the chicken business, with a two-story chicken house in back of their residence.

In front of the store was a bench for the loafers, and on the north side there was a blacksmith shop, where a lot of local machinery probably got repaired. It also held a pot-bellied stove where the winter loungers sat and spit their tobacco. They were supposed to spit into a sand-filled coal bucket but generally spit on the side of the stove causing it to sizzle. Pat said it made her mother furious, which is probably why they did it.

Inside the front door was a small grocery area with a customer counter, on which sat a huge wheel of longhorn cheese, sold by the pound. Harry kept an ice house there too, in which he held perishable foods like meat, milk, and the like. I can still bring up the taste of liver cheese my mom bought there, which I loved (although I can't abide the taste of liver now). The ice was cut into approximately one-foot chunks, and an ice pick was used to chip off pieces as needed. The ice also served to cool the red soda (pop) cooler with the opener screwed to the outside that held Coca Cola and other pop flavors like orange, grape, and Baker's strawberry, the best strawberry drink ever made.

And last, but not the least interesting, was the big cage on the north side in which he housed raccoons. These animals were trapped and brought to Harry by some of the more entrepreneurial natives, and were held there until it was time for a 'coon hunt at the IOOF lodge. Someone would take the caged animals and release them at the appropriate time to provide the dogs a trail to tree; not a tale our SPCA and PETA friends like to hear, but a fact of life in rural Missouri, even now. It may make my readers feel better to know that a good many got away, but the rest probably provided some much appreciated income (and equally important bragging rights) for the hunters.

Fink's Store

Early historical descriptions of Avalon include mention of a hotel. As I was looking through old photos in my mom's collection, I found some that at first, I wasn't sure were of the same building. The upstairs showed a set of double doors that opened onto a railed deck which was the roof of the porch, the supporting posts of which were somewhat ornate. I realized this was probably the hotel. There was also a sign on the building that said "Browning." The Browning family was prominent in the community at one time, owning a bank and also having built the house I grew up in.

To the right in a couple of photos, a building was visible, set back to the south, which appeared to be a barn, perhaps a livery for the horses which would have been a main source of transportation before the turn of the century. It may have been patronized by guests traveling to Avalon for local events such as fairs, tent revivals, Chataquas at the Avalon College, and horse races. Elmer Kerr, a well-known local judge and politician, owned a race track on land just west of town where harness races were held.

In 1910 the building was purchased by Frank Fink, who operated a mercantile store. His son, E.W., inherited the store and in turn, it then passed to his son, Leland. I recall Leland and Dell Fink as an old and genteel couple when I was growing up, both with snow white hair. Della's hair was always beautifully coiffed with gentle waves. Fink's emporium sat on the south side of the blacktop across from June's store. It was a rather beautiful building, painted white in those days, two stories high, with lots of windows and a grand cement porch across the front.

On the east side of the building was a narrow chicken coop which supplied Avalonians with both eggs and fresh chickens for Sunday dinner.

Inside, the downstairs was split into two rooms, with one entrance opening to the side where groceries and sundries could be bought. The other room, accessed through a second entrance or through an interior pass-through door, was a treasure house of dry goods, including fabrics and sewing notions as well as shoes and clothing. I recall all three walls, side and back, with floor-to-ceiling shelves filled with hats and shoes, and counters or tables covered with bolts of cloth, overalls, shirts, socks and underwear, and whatever else happened to be stocked. I don't recall as a child being much interested by that room.

But what did draw me into the store was the display case with all the candy a child could buy for a penny, nickel, or dime. Not much in those days cost a quarter, but we usually had a coin or two to spend and that was the only place to do it. Attesting to their eternal allure and popularity, a lot of these candies are still around. Double Bubble gum, licorice twists, peppermints, Tootsie Rolls and Tootsie Roll Pops, Milk Duds, Hersey, Milky Way, Snickers, Payday and Three Musketeers bars, as well as temporary exotics like flying saucer-shaped wafer sandwich things with little dot candies that rattled, something like today's Pixie Sticks, candy cigarettes, and a bunch more I can't name.

It's a good thing I never had much money to spend or I would have been fat as a tick and sick as a dog on a regular basis, and with rotten teeth.

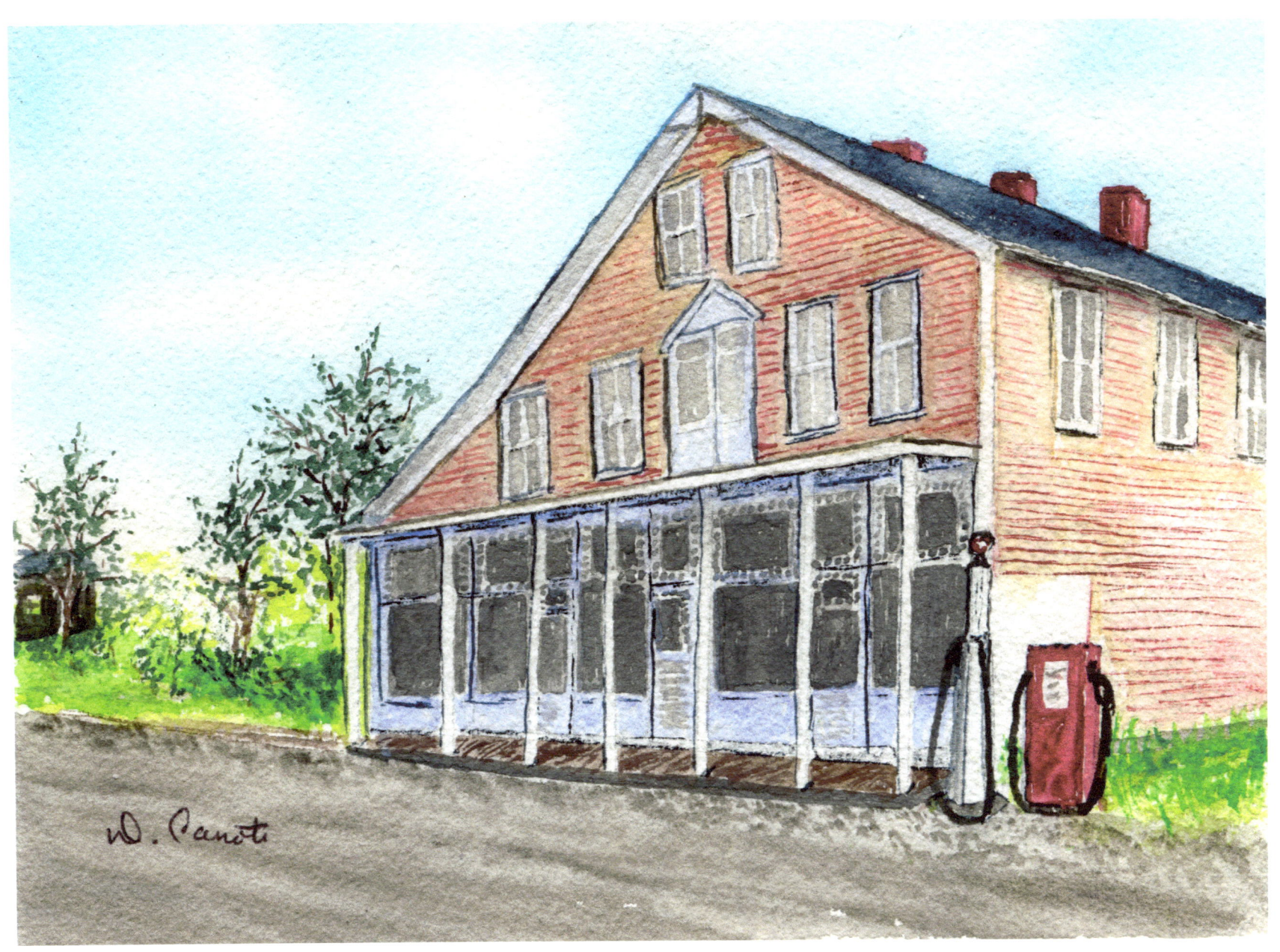

June's Store

This building started out as Bob Shield's store, selling yet more grocery and dry goods, but when I was growing up it was owned by June Johnson. Some details about the grocery, pool hall, and upstairs so-called recreation room where dances and poker games were held, as well as the meat locker plant on the south side were described in my earlier book. As I was thinking about this, I realized there are probably a bunch of folks who have no idea what a meat locker is.

For those not familiar with this facility, before wide-spread rural electrification most homes had no way to preserve meats after butchering other than salting or smoking. While home canning of fruits, vegetables, and even some meats was a standard practice for most rural communities, long-term storage of meats was more problematic. And keep in mind I'm not talking about *now*, I'm describing the situation in days of yore before refrigerated storage was available to all.

Other than the occasional need for a chicken dinner or a celebratory hog roast or barbeque, butchering was not a year-round activity. Rather, it depended on seasonal temperatures, cycles of breeding, birthing (or hatching), and raising meat animals to slaughter size. Roosters get feisty and hens go 'broody' at specific times and if you wanted to hatch a bunch of poultry you would do that at the optimal season. Likewise, hogs and cattle, and sheep if you happened to keep the woollies, were fattened throughout the summer grazing season and slaughtered in late fall or early winter after it becomes cold enough for flies and spoilage not to be such a problem.

Thanks to FDR's Rural Electrification Act (REA) in 1936, Avalon and other towns in the area received electric service. Small businesses found it economical to install electricity and were able to provide extended frozen storage for those who didn't have it. The frozen food locker was the logical outgrowth of the traditional ice house. In the interest of brevity (and for the reader with a short attention span) a meat locker is simply a walk-in freezer.

After butchering and skinning off-site (i.e. on the farm), the pork or beef carcasses were brought to the locker where they were hung in a refrigerated room to age, then cut up, packaged and stored in a system of large drawers rented by the grocer to customers. One could purchase a whole, a quarter, or a half of a beef or hog and have it stored there until it was needed.

So much for the facility, except for the human interest aspect. June herself was a substantial woman, feisty and not tolerating fools gladly. An astute businesswoman, she was also, at least to me, a warmhearted and generous person. She also tolerated the gang of oldster tobacco spitters (but *never* on the porch!) who held down the Main Street viewing bench on the store's front porch. I loved that deep, roofed porch. It was made of rough, plank boards laid perpendicular to the building, but worn smooth by foot traffic over the years until it was a blessing to small bare feet. It also had cracks between the planks wide enough to allow passage to any loose change falling from the pockets of the spitter-sitters. Ever since I was a child, I still every so often have a dream of crawling under that porch and scooping up pockets of shiny coins, from a nickel to a silver dollar, out of the dust. Ah, the treasures of a young heart.

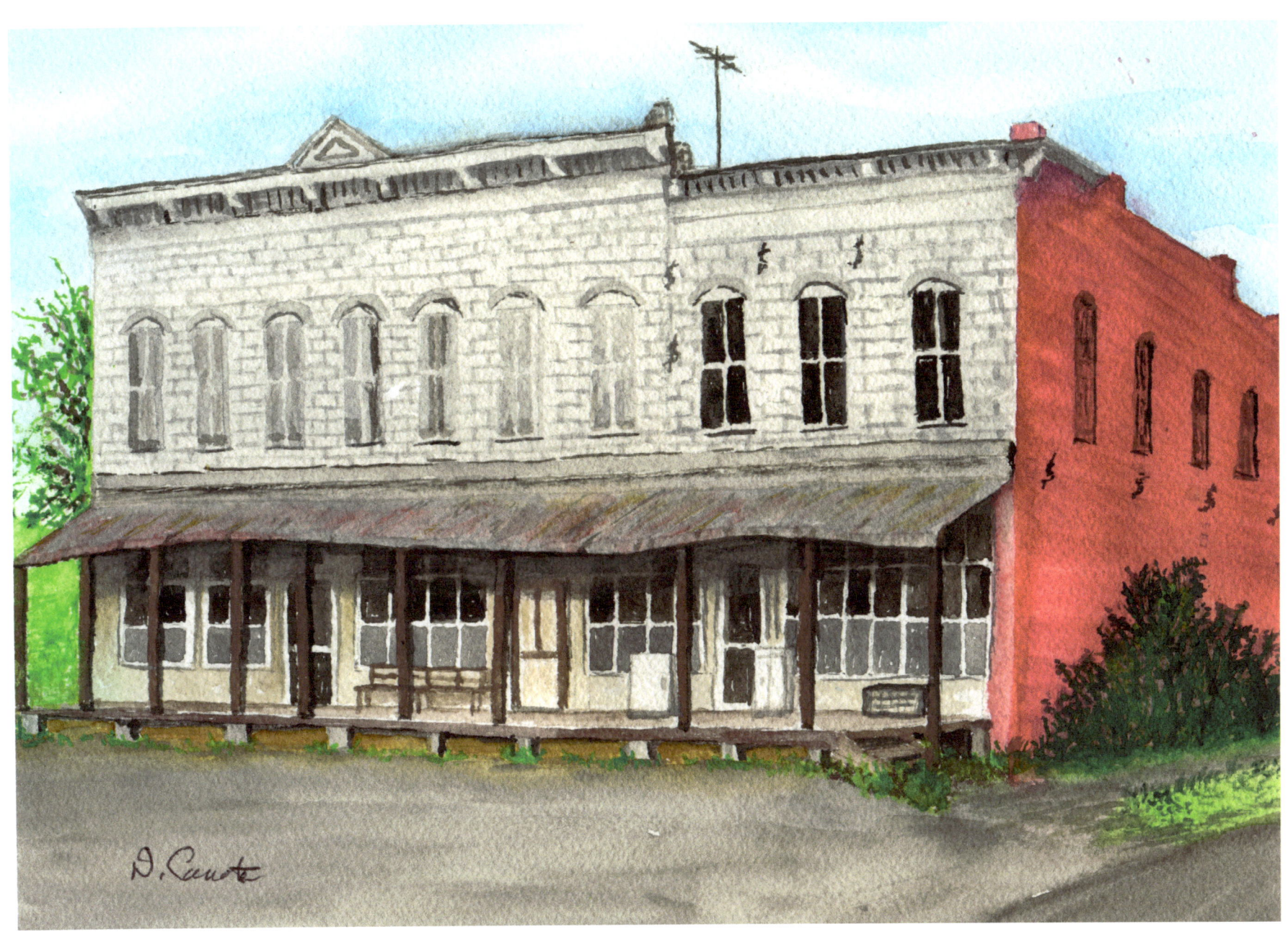

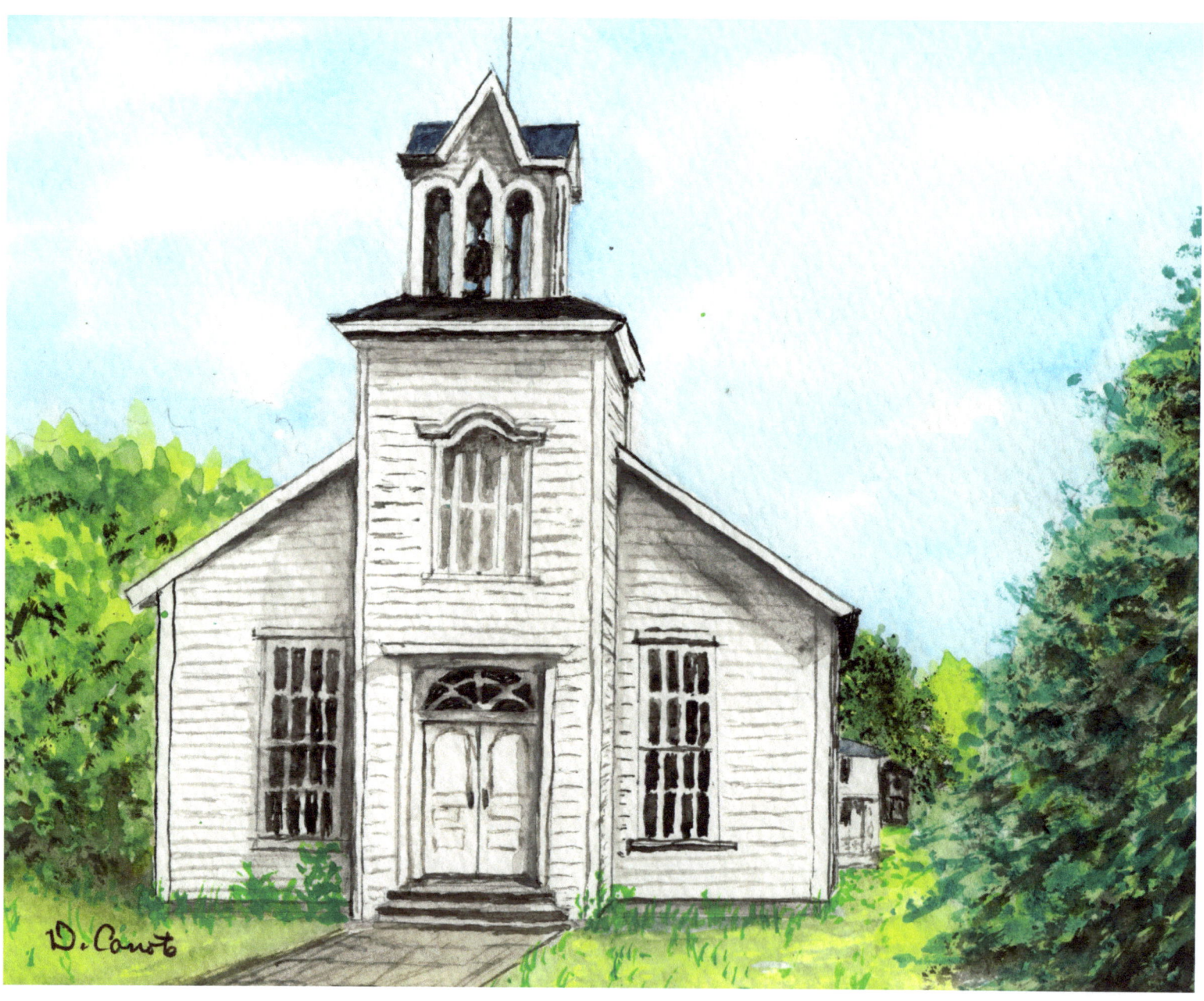

The Avalon Methodist Church

This church building was built by the Presbyterians when they moved to Avalon from their rural location. The Methodists then purchased the building when the Presbyterians bought the Avalon Academy building. The building I painted was from a photo taken in the early 1900s. The belfry on top was insurance that no sinner in town could sleep later than ten o'clock on Sunday morning.

Our house was situated just across the alleyway to the west of the church. While we didn't attend church there, I did see the inside of it on summers when the Methodists alternated with the Presbyterians in holding vacation bible school. Oh the joy of those day-camp experiences! Well, OK, I don't think any of us kids got excited about the bible story part, since we heard those every week at Sunday School. But we had *crafts*, played games, and had *refreshments*—Kool-Aid and cookies! Good stuff! And we learned songs, which weren't a big thrill for some, but I loved music.

So that's the good stuff. Now for some other tales. One involves my big brother, Donald—hunter, gun nut, eventually Marine—and as you know, once a Marine, always a Marine. Don barely escaped involvement with the Chicago gang life when we moved back to Missouri a couple years after I was born. Our dad, a Camel smoker from his teenage years, was terminally ill with lung cancer and we moved back to stay for a time with relatives in Kansas City until he passed away in 1949.

Don's bedroom was upstairs on the east side of the house, and he had a clear shot at the pigeons that frequented the church belfry. His contention was that some of the church-goers mentioned they would not be averse to him ridding them of the source of a considerable amount of pigeon poop. On the other hand, my mom heard the other side of the issue when the women came into the Post Office complaining of the bird carcasses on the sidewalk on Sunday morning. It probably would have remained unresolved except that Don mostly didn't bother to remove the window screen when he went on a shooting spree, and that really teed my mom off. I don't recall the threats she made but the pigeon assassinations ended.

One final story on a less positive note.

As the building aged and its upkeep became more effort and expense than the congregation was willing to put out, they decided to tear it down and build a new, more modern one. I recall a visit to our house by several of the church deacons that just about started World War III. It seems the deacons had decided to install a bathroom in the church basement. Reflecting on this, I don't know where they got their water, since at that time there was no rural water, so all of Avalon's homes used either a well or cisterns. But the issue was the septic tank.

All septic tanks in town, for those that had them, had to have a drainage outlet, which outlet was inevitably into a roadside ditch. Our own tank, located in the back yard, drained into the ditch along the road west of our house.

For those who don't know much about septic tanks, the effluent, which you might expect to be offensive, is not so bad if the tank is working properly. So when the church fellows said they planned to run the outflow pipe under our driveway and have it empty into the ditch a short ways past the front of the house, my mom's eyes got about the size of a quarter and she swelled up (I swear I saw smoke wafting out of her ears) like Vesuvius about to erupt.

You might think it was the effluent that was the problem, which it sorta was, but it was more the issue of the driveway that set her off. For years since we moved there she spent a great deal of money (for us) and effort to fix the driveway entrance, which tended to develop a rut and subsequent rough entry that was hard on cars. It wasn't just the information so much as the arrogant attitude with which it was delivered—a done deal—that set her off.

I guess she gave them an ear-full about repairing the damage they intended to do, and they were not at all consoling or conciliatory in their response. Then, when one of the cads quipped snidely that they would be grading the dirt up around the foundation and all the water would run off on our side anyway, well that did it. Her comment later was, "And here were all those purportedly Christian men who were supposed to take care of the widows and the orphans, and they treat me like this!"

Suffice it to say that this good Christian woman did not thereafter say many prayers for the Methodists—at least not those Methodists.

Chapter 2
Flights of Fancy

We got these old songs in our head from way back. It's like in the movies—they play in the background of our lives, black and white. We got the same music going on in our heads.

—Trudy van Boyce, *Out of the Blue*

When it comes to things, I am an organizer. I write my shopping lists in order by their location in a store. I make my errand list in order of where I have to shop, based on the most efficient route. I am borderline OCD when I have small tasks to do like brushing teeth, climbing stairs and have to count, how many brushes on each side, how many steps, you get the idea. Packing my suitcase, and then my car for a trip, what will I need to get out first? It all used to drive my friends and family crazy. And at the end, it always turns out that something is left out.

That's what this chapter is—the leftovers, the odds and ends, the things I thought about when my mind got really restless to write one more, one more. These essays and paintings don't really fit into the theme of any of the other chapters, but I couldn't bear to leave them behind.

Point of View

We are currently in a news cycle such that every news feed, every radio and TV broadcast, print and online newspaper, magazine, and every live discussion focuses on the COVID-19 pandemic. As of the date of this writing, this country and the world are in its clutches, and everyone is heartily sick and tired of the whole business. Anything I might have to say is probably redundant, but I can't help but reflect on the human condition and on our past history and the short memory and inattention of a population that leads them to gasp in surprise that such a thing could happen in our modern world.

When I was born in 1946 the memory and experiences of my own family were not that far removed in time from the so-called "Spanish Flu" epidemic of the early 1900s. As I was growing up, the mid-twentieth century was just beginning to embrace widespread vaccinations and use of antibiotics, and the chemical industry was taking off in a big way. Childhood diseases like polio, diphtheria, and whooping cough, insect and water-borne diseases like cholera and typhoid, while still common in backwater and third-world countries, were becoming rarer in the United States and other more advanced countries. I was born at a fortunate junction in time between the memories of my grandparents and their world, and the start of today's technology.

Now that the baby boomers are becoming extinct we are losing the memory and stories from that generation, and with that loss we are further removed from the realities of our existence. Just like the Midwest floods of the early 1990s, when Mother Nature flushed the big upstream toilet, we are now smacked in the face with the fact that in spite of our superior engineering and technology we are not invulnerable to the larger truths of nature and biology. Adaptation and evolution follow continual change in the environment, and it is only the realities of our place in that process that need be reconsidered.

So what am I talking about with all this highfalutin discussion? There are always disasters looming on our horizon, and there are always people who understand and predict the potential for such disasters. If we watch and listen to what's going on in the world we can make some informed choices in who we elect to public office. We can think about how to order our lives based not on politics but on building our readiness to deal with disasters while we go through the process of simple daily living. I firmly believe in the courage and resiliency of the American people, and on their overall goodness and humanity, and I embrace and celebrate our diversity of race, ethnicity, and cultures. However we came by this, and in spite of the less than humane conditions and practices that have led up to it, our strength as a nation is a function of this diversity.

When you look at the paintings that accompany this particular essay you may figuratively scratch your head and wonder what it has to do with the writing. I did have something in mind when I did the paintings, something whimsical and nebulous. But since then I have periodically looked at them again, and every time I do I see something else in them.

Unlike my other musings, I am not going to give you an interpretation. If we ever have occasion to meet or otherwise communicate, I would very much like to hear your thoughts.

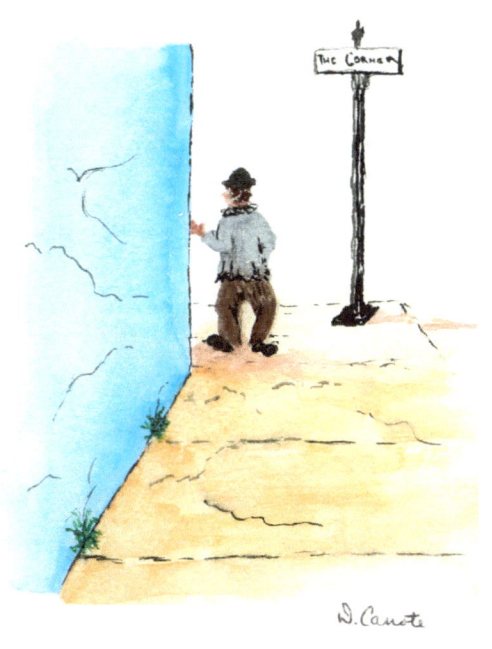

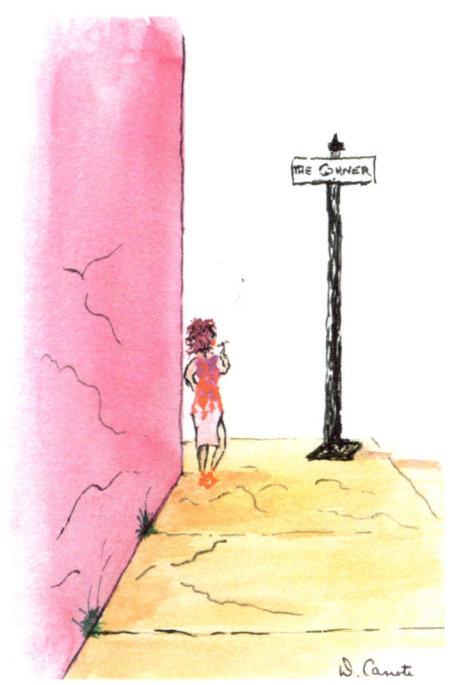

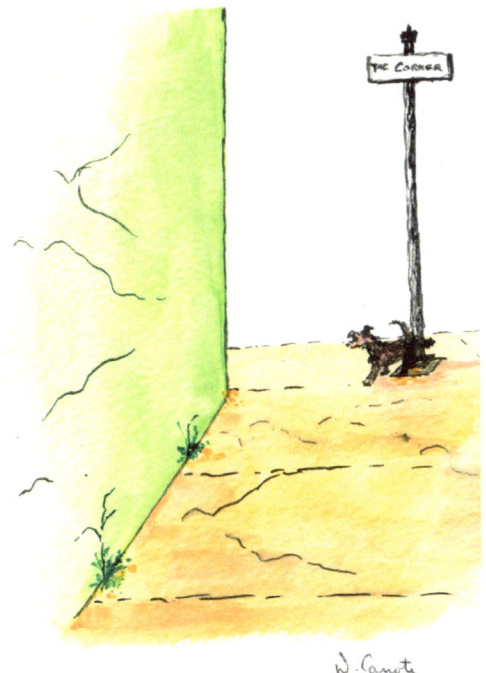

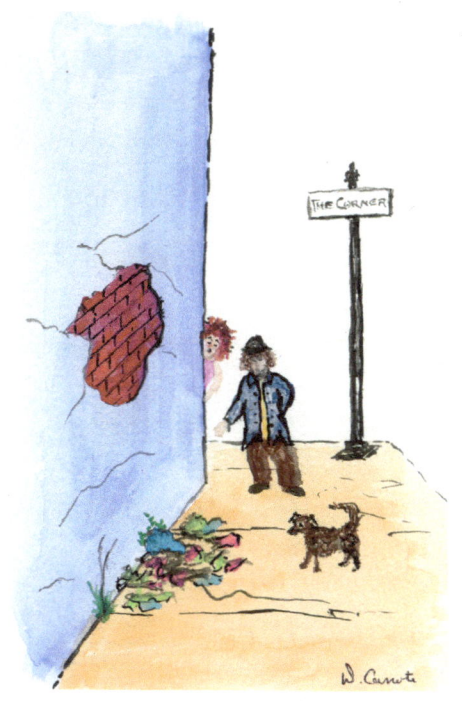

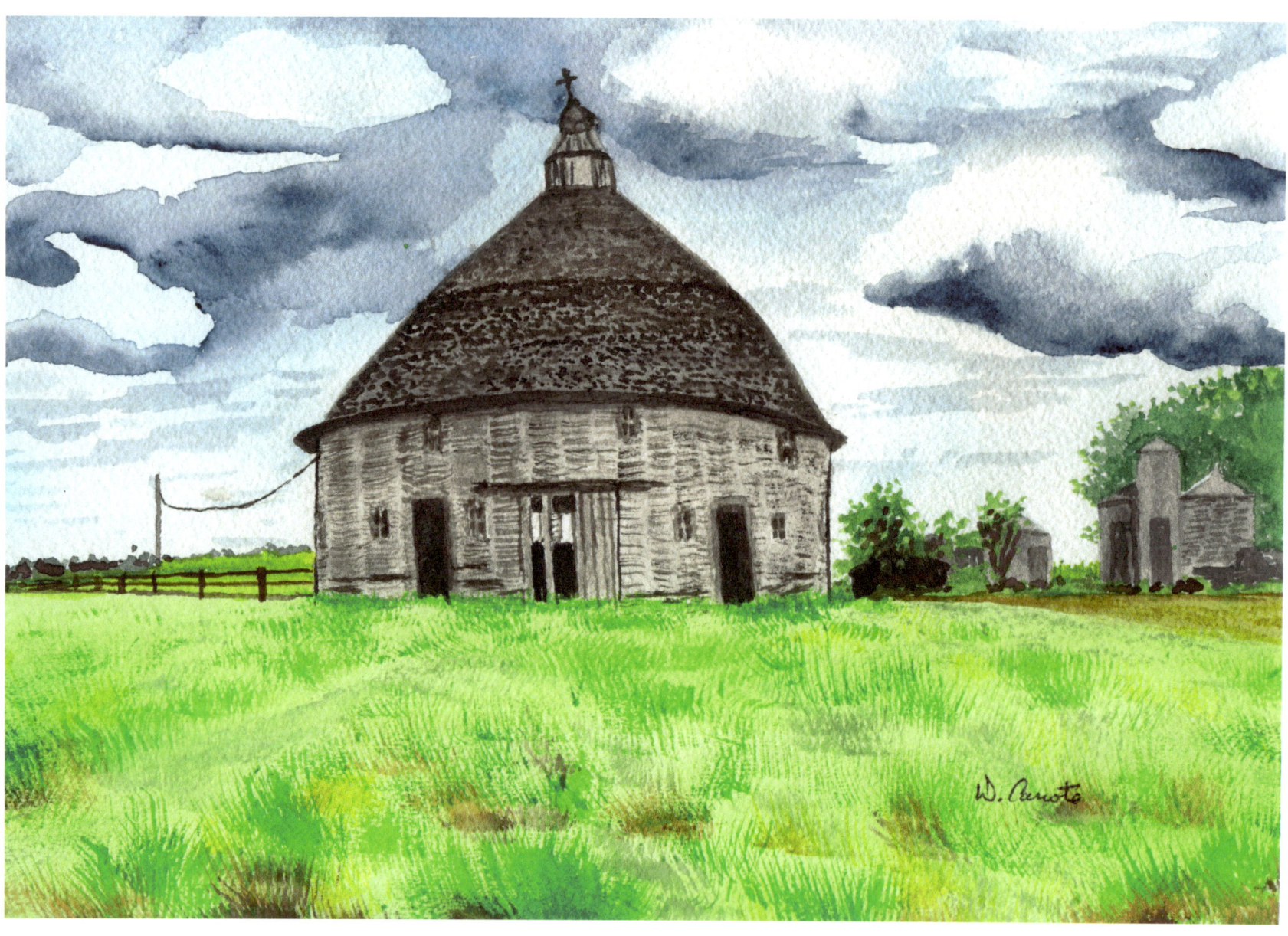

The Round Barn

This barn sits near a blacktop road in northern Carroll County, Missouri. I was taking an alternative route north from my home in Harrisburg on my way to visit a childhood friend who lives on Highway 65 in southern Livingston County. I had seen the barn on a previous trip and had plenty of time and the kind of nice overcast day that is conducive to good photos. The structure was just rough enough to meet my criteria of old and interesting.

Once I started researching round barns I began to appreciate why I hadn't seen more of them. This design is one of truly American origin, starting with Shakers in western Massachusetts. As migrants settled farther west, the design was undoubtedly brought with them and enjoyed a certain popularity in a number of Midwestern states. The period of their construction is primarily through the nineteenth and early twentieth centuries and they were popular with dairymen in Wisconsin and Illinois. They were also common farther west in the middle plains states from the Dakotas through Kansas, as their design was considered to be more practical and resilient under the windy, stormy conditions common there.

Round barns were also stronger and more economical of materials, constructed by tension and stress framing, with mortise and tenon joining rather than pegs, nails, or screws. Balloon framing used lighter, more closely placed studs in place of the large timber-framed members used in rectangular barns, and the unique circular design of the round barn roof did not require the support of joists. It was also easier to handle animals in a round barn, as there were no corners for them to bunch up into.

This particular characteristic—the lack of corners—has stuck in my memory, as I had once been on an otherwise unmemorable drive with my brother Don as we passed this same barn.

A man of few words, when he did talk about something he usually had some pithy kernel of wisdom to impart, so when he informed me that the barn was where a man had gone crazy, I turned eagerly to him and said, "Yeah?"

"Yes," he nodded soberly, "he went crazy trying to find a corner to piss in." Sucker....

But indeed, as I did some research on this topic, the topic of a person not being able to find a corner did come up several times, although no one commented on its significance. Now we know.

If you are interested in the topic of round barns, I heartily recommend Jacqueline Dougan Jackson's book, *Stories from the Round Barn*, based on her life on a Wisconsin dairy farm. For a factual and pictorial treatment of the subject, I recommend the article by James R. Shortridge, "The Round Barns of Kansas," which can be found in the archives of the Kansas Historical Society.

Stalking the Wily Mushroom

The topic of fungi came up at a brunch with a serendipitously merged group of plant enthusiasts. Our Backyard Herb Group and the Missouri Native Plant Society were seated together at Uprise Bakery in Columbia. We were trying to break through a temporary hiatus of our herb club's activities, our club's founder and leader (me) having spent the past year trying to come to terms with the aging process. One member of our group was enthusing about the film she had just seen, *Fantastic Fungi*, which reminded me of my own enthusiasm for the topic of fungi. Remembering some of my previous mushroom paintings, I resolved to include them in my next group of writings.

There are probably as many opinions about mushrooms as there are kinds of mushrooms, and that would be quite a lot. They didn't figure much in my mother's cooking, so as a child I never learned to appreciate their culinary properties. However, like many kids and a considerable number of adults, I always considered toadstools to be pretty cool. It wasn't until well into my college years when I began to appreciate the fact that I could sneak them into my diet, thanks to my undergraduate major professor at Missouri Valley College.

Dr. Mike Wirth was something beyond my previous experience. Slender, bearded, and with a wry cynical manner, his typical classroom attire was bib overalls, sandals (no socks), and whatever shirt he wore was not memorable. He and his wife lived within a couple blocks of the courthouse square in Marshall, along with two tropical owls, seven Siamese cats, and an alligator in the back yard in a small shallow pool interspersed between pot plants. We're talking 1966, and hippydom, having barely worked its way to the Midwest, was not a familiar concept, so he managed to elude the attention of the powers that be. Top that off with an ancient beat-up Volkswagen Beetle with rusting paint, plastic flowers in the headlights, and no floor in the back seat and you have an idea of how cool he was considered by all his students.

Botany class was one of my favorites, and when we got to the topic of fungi, it included several forays into the countryside for collection trips. Since our farm was located within only a few miles of campus, I volunteered our several acres of back woods as a destination. We carpooled out there one day after an early spring rain. Dr. Wirth was well versed in the edible varieties and we located quite a few, including one group that became a life-long favorite.

Of course, most folks who read this will think of the wild morel, the one and only thing that will get my husband to take a walk in the woods. The price people sell these for is obscene; however there is always someone willing to spend it for the pleasure of this culinary experience. Those who are willing to tramp through the woods and fields to pick their own may be rewarded with garbage bags full or, in some years, none at all. They also fervently guard the secret of their favorite hunting grounds with wicked stares and closed lips. My husband James swears they pop up behind him after he passes. When given the chance, he will make an entire meal of only morels.

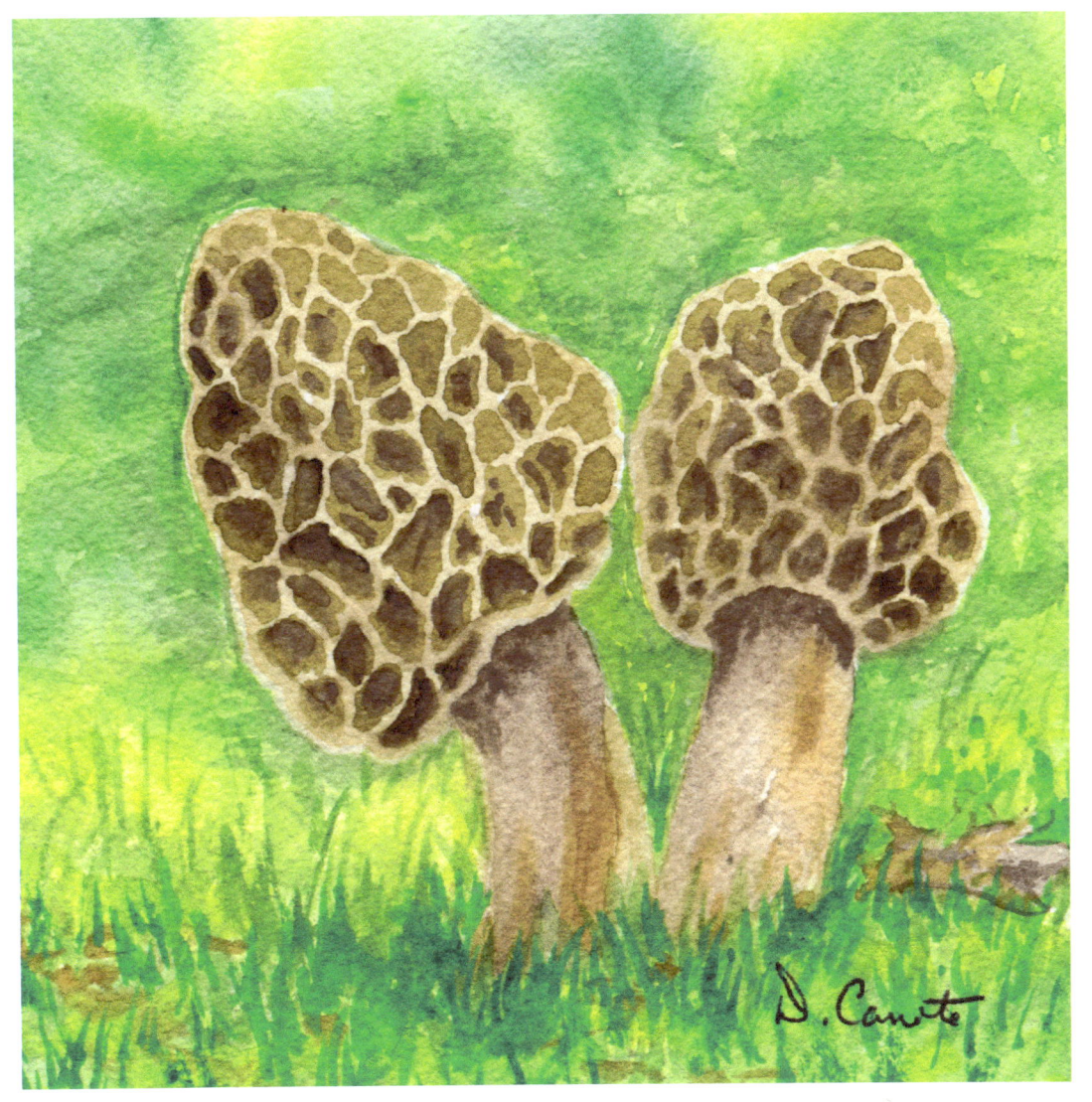

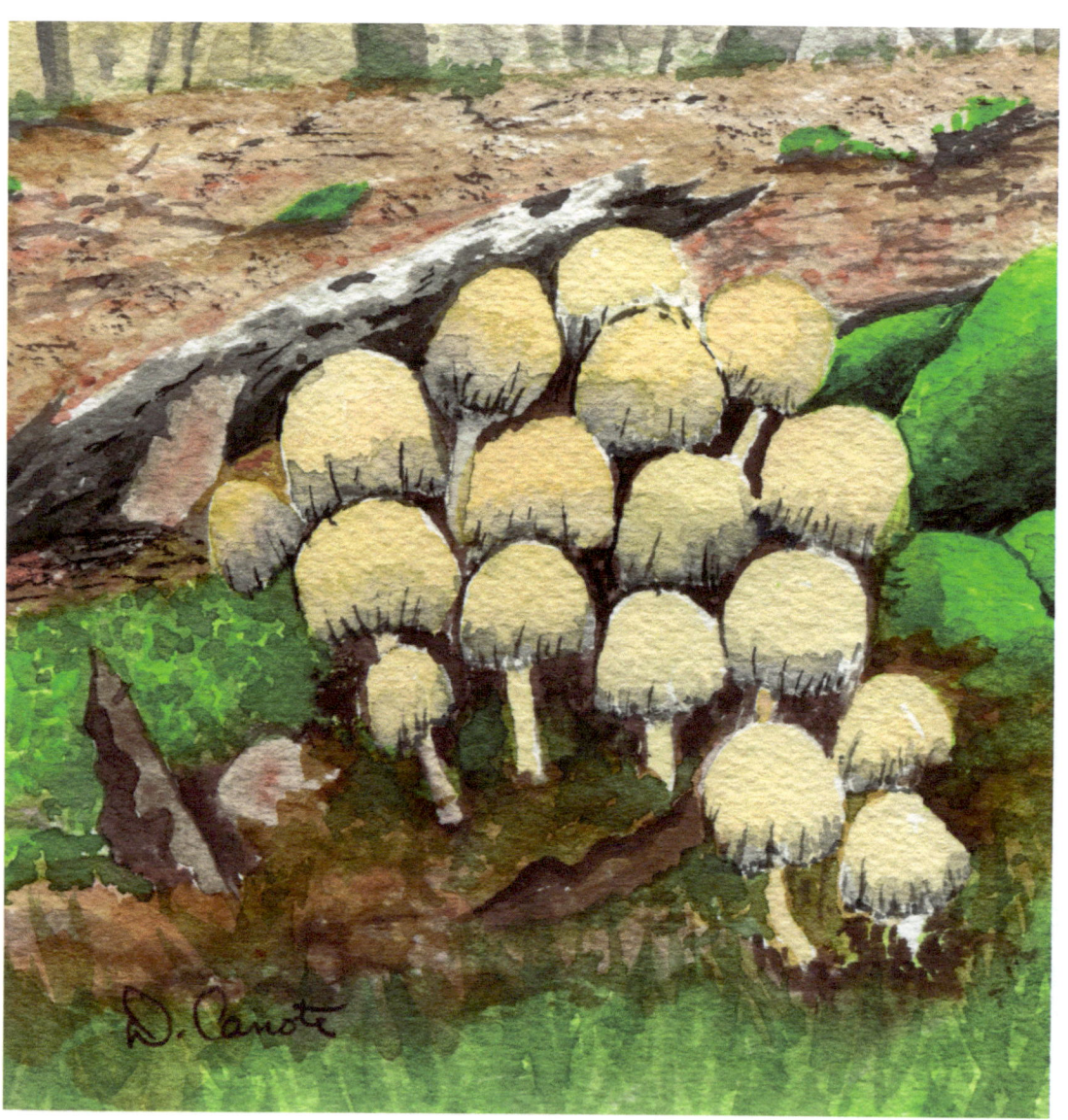

But thanks to my college days I have one that I like equally well. The fungal family Coprinaceae includes several common mushroom species, collectively known as inky caps as a consequence of their self-digesting enzymes that turn them into a black slimy mess.

Coprinus atramentarius and *Coprinus micaceus* are small and are fairly common here in Missouri. They are usually found in the cool wet conditions of early spring and or late fall. They arise in clumps around old tree stumps or buried wood, and the spore-bearing masses of fruiting bodies, i.e. mushrooms, last only a day or two. Appearing for only two or three years at any location, the masses of mushrooms come up farther and farther away from the tree stumps as the underground mycelium breaks down and exhausts the nutrient supply from the rotting roots. *Coprinus comatus*, shaggy mane, is a larger mushroom, and often appears in grassy lawns in the spring and summer presenting the appearance of brilliant white phallic shoots several inches tall that open into disc-like platforms up to six or eight inches in diameter.

Shaggy mane toadstool is big enough to support even the largest toad. It is considered the choicest and most desirable Coprinus, having greater size and thus providing more food mass. However, I much prefer the smaller inky caps. If you discover a clump right after they emerge, the best way to collect them is to slice through the stems of the mass with a sharp knife at ground level, avoiding the dirt and leaves around them. The caps are somewhat fragile, so if they are collected carefully and cleanly, little washing is needed. Sautéed in a little butter until they change to a more translucent limp condition, they are best served atop a saltine cracker with a little sprinkle of salt on top. Divine!

One last warning, however, about trying the inky cap. *Coprinus atramentarius* is also known as tippler's bane, and consuming it with alcohol can cause facial reddening, nausea, vomiting, palpitations, and tingling limbs. Extreme cases have been know to lead to heart attack. So, if you're a tippler, beware the wily inky cap.

My Love Affair with Water

I was born near the cusp of both Aquarius and Pisces, so naturally I love water! It is the single most important molecule on earth, without which we would have no atmosphere, no oceans or other water bodies, and of course no plant or animal life.

Think of how good it feels to emerge from a shower or bath or even a swim: clean, invigorated, more prepared to face the next challenge life will slap in our faces. Think of those clean clothes coming out of the laundry; the dog, free of the evidence of the wonderful dead or fecal remains it rolled in; your car or truck, minus the dust and mud from the road and the bird poo from the tree you parked under. I'm sure you can add other great uses of water to my list.

I love the first rains of spring that activate the smell of the actinomycete, *Streptomyces*, which produces that fresh earthy scent. I love the lightening and thunder of a good thunderstorm and the gentle warm rains of summer, the cool rainy days that follow summer, in which the clouds and moisture heighten the colors of autumn leaves and enhance the scent of burned leaves.

My love affair started when I was a child, wading in the roadside ditches of Avalon. There were creatures in the water there that only appeared in the spring when the ditches ran full, and were calling me to catch them ("Dorothy..., Dorothy..."). My mom was pretty tolerant when I brought them home and put them in a jar of water, but always made me take them back in a day or two. Bless you, Mom, for your forbearance.

I also had a favorite hike to a small creek north of town, just perfect for safe wading, which sometimes had small fish, crawdads, and tadpoles. I also discovered wonderfully interesting rocks and fossils that found their way home in my pockets. Those stayed around a little longer than the live captives, but still disappeared eventually.

I have a tremendous respect, even some fear, for the power of moving water and the deep presence of large water bodies. Once I got over the trauma of water up my nose and learned to swim properly, I swam in everything available, from weedy, muddy farm ponds to the briny ocean at Galveston, from cold crystal Ozark streams to the Great Salt Lake. On our senior class 'sneak day' about half our class (ten or so) played hooky from school, meeting at dawn and piling into two cars. We started the day with a sunrise visit to Swan Lake, a hike at Pershing Park to see the champion cottonwood tree, a picnic lunch, a visit to Mandeville lake which involved a swim (in swim suits of course), and ending with a movie at Chillicothe's drive-in theater. Since we didn't have enough money between us to get everyone in, two or three snuck in, stuffed in the trunk.

When I related the day's events to my mom, she looked at me in alarm and stated, "They say there's no bottom to Mandeville Lake!" To which I nonchalantly replied, "Well, we only swam on the top."

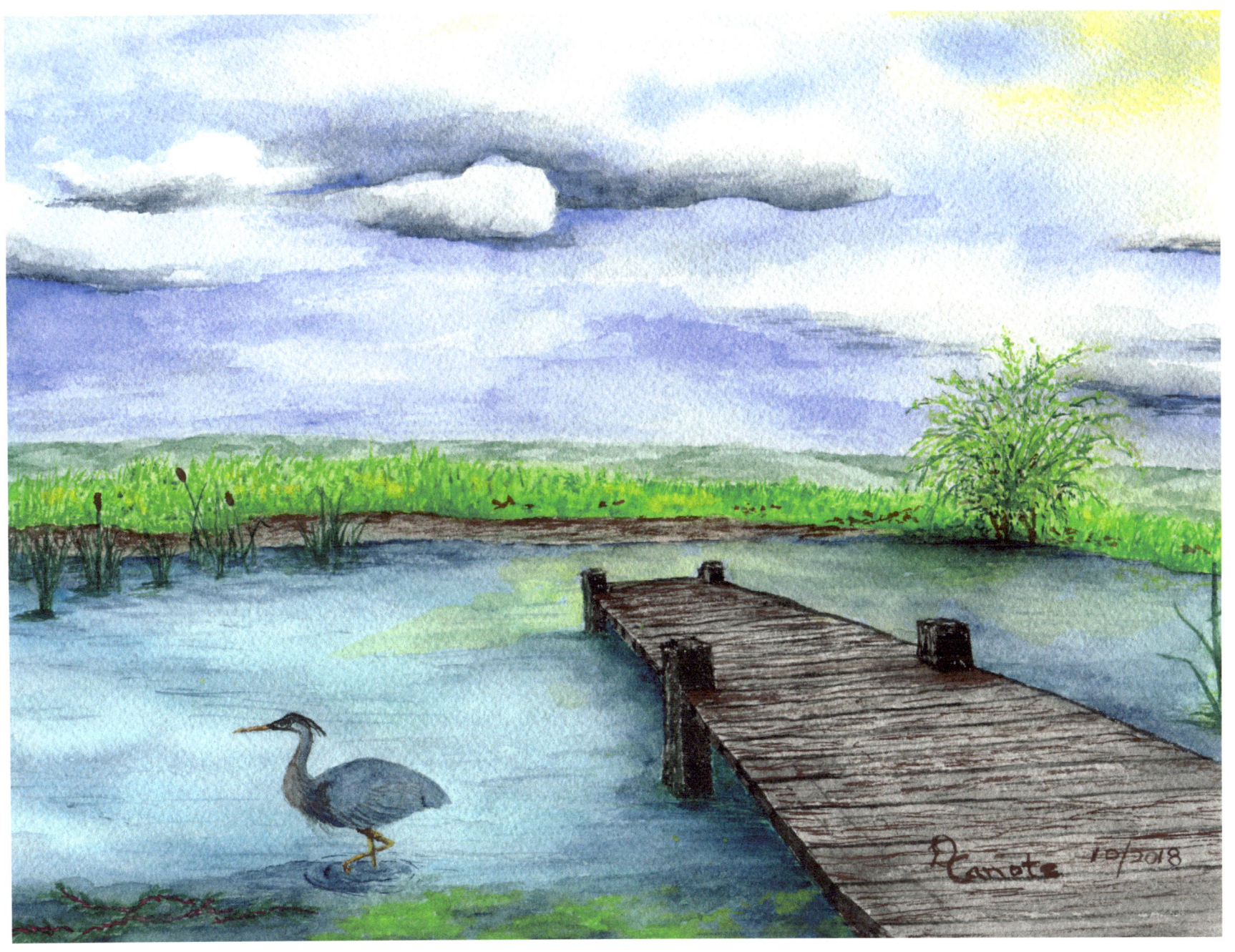

My Love Affair with the Southwest

At some point in the middle years I started a love affair with the southwest. The first trips were into Texas to visit my daughters who had moved to Austin with their dad while I was in grad school. Traveling in Texas was like being in a whole different country.

Growing up in Missouri, surrounded by the rolling hills and prairies of the north and the hills and hollers of the Ozarks, did not prepare me for the absolute flatness and visual distances as I drove south through Kansas and Oklahoma and into Texas. Later travels into New Mexico made me more interested in the landscapes and the people, and while I will probably never travel as much again, I still have dreams of the desert.

Utah

Before I get too far south, I have to say a bit about a trip to Utah. I was visiting some of my fellow scientists, field biologists from the federal fisheries lab in Columbia, who were doing toxicity studies on the flame retardants dropped on wildfires by planes.

They were at the end of their study and had made some recreational plans prior to returning to Missouri. These included a hike up into the Uinta Mountains, and a raft trip down a section of the Green River. Whew, that was a hoot! "High side! Everybody hug the rock!"

We were so close to Dinosaur National Monument that we stopped in there and checked out the bones in the side of the mountain. Before it was uplifted, that part of the country was characterized by rivers, which carried the bones, dumped them there, and them buried them in the alluvia, eventually becoming sandstone and conglomerate rocks. The Visitors Center there is built attached to the side of the rocky slope where fossilized bones are exposed and can actually be touched by visitors.

But the most memorable part of the trip was an accidental discovery as we were out driving around. A sign beside the road directed the way to the Josie Morris Cabin. We decided to check it out.

A little ways along the side road we came to a tiny cabin situated at the mouth of a box canyon. It was fenced to prevent trespass, so we weren't able to enter, but could see through the windows to parts of the interior. Crudely furnished, it was quite picturesque but I wondered about the woman, Josie Morris, for which it was named.

At the Visitors Center I happened on a book (I have to bring one home from every trip) entitled, *The Bassett Women*. This story related the background for Josie Morris and her family, contemporaries of the Hole in the Wall Gang and Butch Cassidy, her sister's purported beau. Outliving three husbands, Josie lived alone in her cabin until 1963 and passed away at the age of eighty-nine in 1964, the same year I graduated from high school. She was a testament to the hardiness and tenacity of the western women of her time. This book remains one of my favorite go-tos when I have exhausted all the other reading matter in my house.

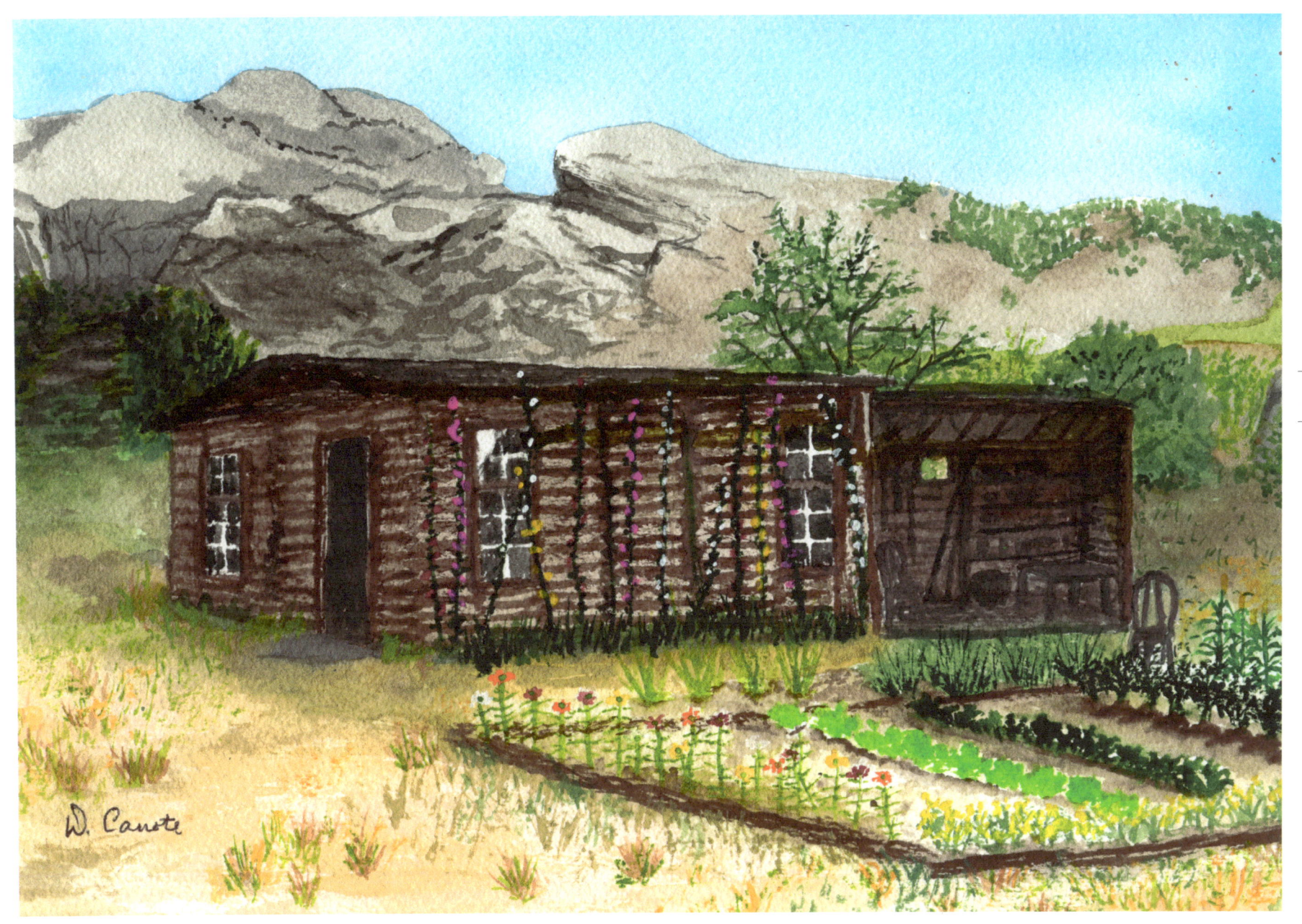

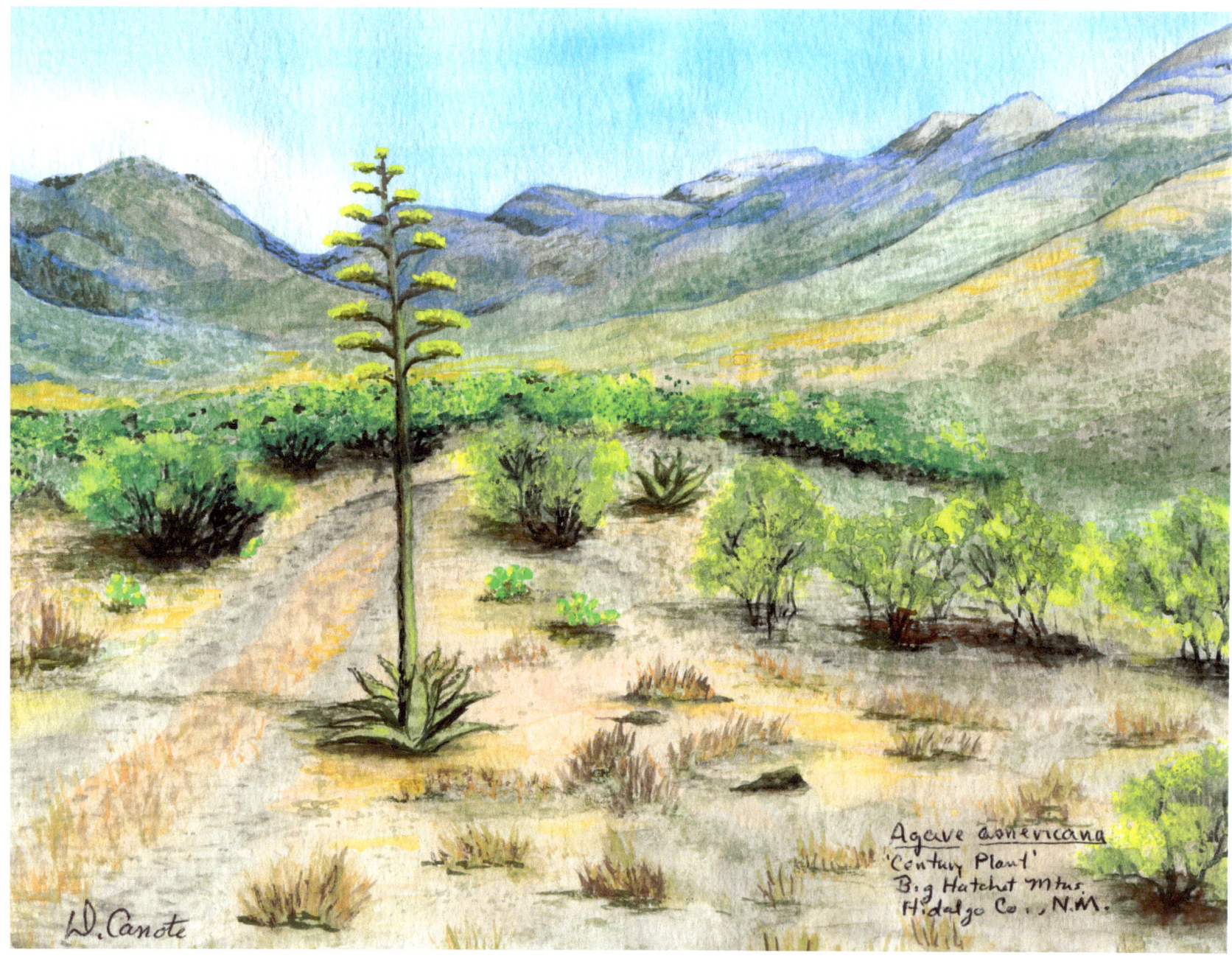

Agave americana
'Century Plant'
Big Hatchet Mtns.
Hidalgo Co., N.M.

D. Canote

New Mexico

I have been on several trips to New Mexico for various and sundry reasons. The most recent was to visit my daughter Angela during her time at the University of New Mexico (UNM) in Albuquerque. I wrote about this trip/adventure in my first book so won't say any more about that.

Prior to that I had two other occasions to visit the state. The first was a visit to a friend who was working on his PhD at UNM-El Paso. That trip covered a visit to White Sands National Park and Carlsbad Caverns, both obviously impressive in totally different ways. But the most memorable part of the trip was an afternoon and evening jaunt across the border with friends to Ciudad Juarez. Starting with some shopping and tasty taquitos from a street vendor, we followed that by an evening meal at the Virginia Club. At one time, Juarez was reported to have a restaurant for each state it the United States, catering to military personnel from Fort Bliss.

I was at that time a novice at Mexican cuisine but knew enough to request the mildest dishes on the menu. Let me just say that the dining staff and the so-called friends had a great deal of entertainment out my reaction to the mild salsa. Bunch of (expletive deleted) chili heads, no doubt they are still dining out on that tale.

My second trip to New Mexico was with my friend Jamin (Thomas) Bray to Taos. This little town, about an hour and a half north of Santa Fe, has an interesting history as an artist's mecca. We were there as an excuse for a road trip. We drove west on a diversion to send some shouts up Echo Canyon where we were advised to avoid the ground squirrels and other rodents that carried the hantavirus. We visited the market square in Santa Fe but didn't buy much, as we were poor at that time. We took a drive up to Taos Pueblo and wandered around gawking like the tourists we were.

But the interesting part was the place we camped out. We were in my truck and had hauled most everything we needed to avoid the expense of a motel, and Jamin located a little campground and trading post a little ways out of Taos. We were both unattached at the time and were delighted to find the trading post operator and a friend who provided campfire entertainment. That's all I will say about that.

On the way back, we stopped in Springfield so Jamin could be reunited with her truck. I left there heading toward home, but finally gave out and had to catch some sleep at an I-44 rest stop. When I eventually came to, there was a sign under my windshield wiper with the words, "Wake me up, Thelma, and lets roll!"

Texas

First, let me tell you a story from a trip that you will read about in Chapter Four, where I talk about my truck. When I was working at ABC Labs, a colleague, Jane Bowman and I had occasion to travel to Houston for a meeting. We were sitting at a picnic table eating that evening and on the table I saw an interesting caterpillar and leaned over to get a better look at it. A young man was also sitting there and said, "Whoa, girl, you want to avoid that critter!" Turns out this one is called an asp. And no, this isn't the notorious snake of the middle east, it is the caterpillar larvae of a moth, actually pretty, with an Elvis hairdo. He proceeded to tell me about the stinging hairs and how bad they hurt.

I recalled this years later when I encountered several in some Georgia cypress mulch I bought from Home Depot to mulch my berry vines. I picked one off the cuff of my glove where it began to itch and before the evening was over my arm had swollen to twice its normal size and hurt all the way to my shoulder. Evidently they are common throughout the southern states and even account for several deaths each year from anaphylactic shock.

And now let me say a few things about my infatuation for the state. Texas has a larger-than-life image of itself, and in my mind I found it to be true. Because of its size, it encompasses a huge diversity of landscapes—from the piney woods and the verdant east through the central blackland prairie, into the karst-dissected hill country, and out into the dry plains and deserts of west Texas.

Ever since it gained its independence from Mexico, Texas has embodied a 'kiss my patootie' ambiance, thumbs its nose at federal wishes and incentives, and could care less what the rest of the forty nine states think about it. When the nationwide speed limit was dropped to fifty five miles per hour and Texas was threatened with the loss of highway funding for noncompliance, Texas decided they didn't need the stinking federal dollars. In fact, their farm-to-market road system is one of the finest I have driven on.

Also, most people are aware that our electrical network throughout the United States is an interconnected grid, like a giant spiderweb receiving from and distributing to all aspects of our infrastructure. There is one system that supplies the eastern states and one that supplies the western states. Except Texas—it has its own darned grid which, by the way, it shares with northern Mexico.

It is hardly necessary to inform my readers of much of the history of Texas. Most of my generation grew up with stories of the Alamo, the Texas Rangers, and Frank Dobie's tales. My Ex and daughters lived in Round Rock, just to the northwest of Austin, and Round Rock had its own folk hero in the person of Sam Bass.

Austin itself is an interesting city noted for, among other things, its horrendous traffic and *Austin City Limits*. I have had reason to visit Austin many times to see my daughter, Angela, and while I don't make the drive in one day as I once did, I still love driving into and through the countryside and morphing into a new persona.

Finally, country and rock music has its share of Texas influence. I won't list all the singer/songwriters I admire, but I still haven't gotten over the loss of Stevie Ray Vaughn and Duane Allman.

Maybe when I die I can be reborn a Texan.

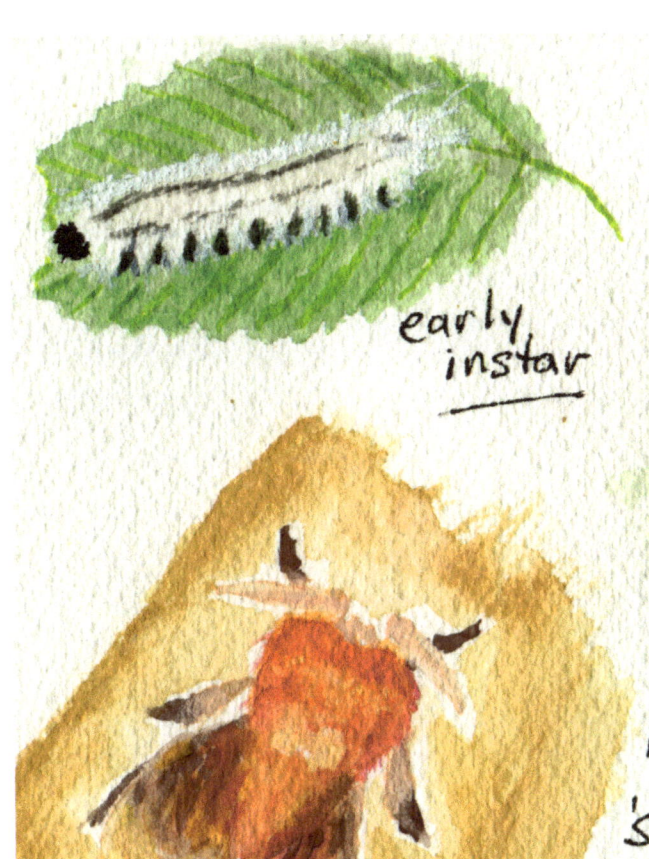

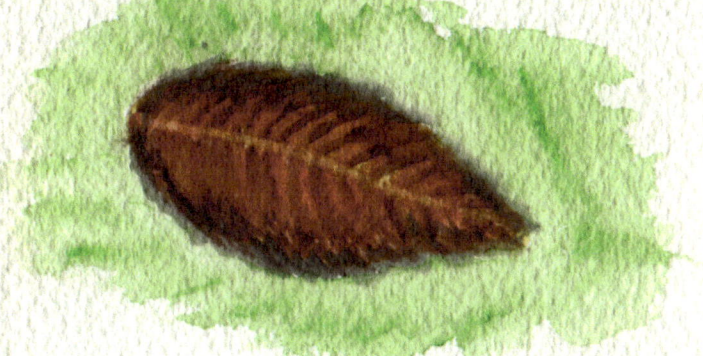

Asp
caterpillar

Megalopyge opercularis

early
instar

late instar

Adult

'Southern flannel moth'
aka 'puss moth'

S. Canote

I always did something I was a little not ready to do. I think that's how you grow. When there's that moment of 'Wow, I'm not really sure I can do this,' and you push through those moments, that's when you have a breakthrough.

—Marissa Mayer

Chapter Three
Walks on the Wild Side

The Concept of Wild

I never really thought about the concept until I started writing for this second book. Wild is a relative term, and subjective, and has to be considered in context. Think about it. "He got a wild idea." "They went out into the wild." "He had wild, curly hair." "She was a wild child." I like the thought that wild implies undomesticated, unorthodox, something other than business as usual.

When you consider the spectrum of human experience and behavior, I would say I was never a wild child, other than perhaps in some of my thinking. A college boyfriend described me as having "a wonderful irreverence for authority," which I consider probably the nicest thing anyone ever told me. I have embraced it wholeheartedly. For me, an adventure is a trip somewhere I had never been, but not one that involves much risk. As a child and adolescent I was a tomboy, but not a daredevil. So maybe I was a bit girly, but hey, I'm a girl!

Several key people in my life have given me advice and encouragement at times when I had doubts about both myself and my decisions. My high school teachers assured me that yes, I should and would do well when I went off to college, although it took me until graduate school before I really learned how to study properly. When I stated my misgivings about the outcome of something I was about to attempt, a good friend during my grad school years told me, "You can do things you don't think you can do."

So as I approached the edge of a cliff in Capon Park, on shaking legs and about to lose my lunch, ready to get on rope for my first rappel, I was assured by my experienced friends and mentors that what others did, I could do also. And I did. That was my first real introduction to adventure. I was ready to go out into the wild.

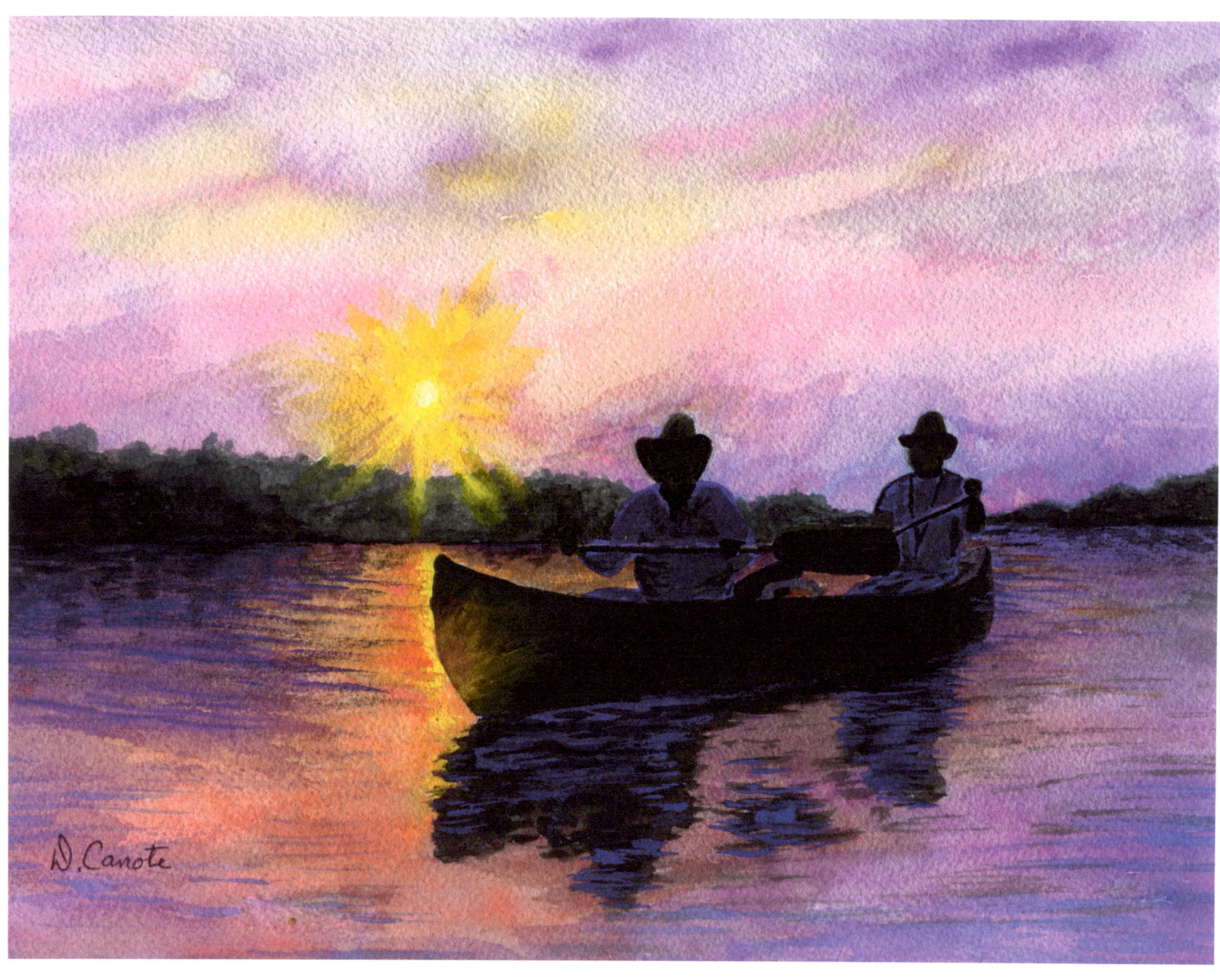

D. Canote

Some New Friends

During my years as a grad student at MU, I made a bunch of acquaintances. Jim Huckins, or Huck as he was known to his friends, was my research mentor. Huck and another friend, Kevin Feltz were research chemists at the federal environmental research lab on the southern outskirts of Columbia. When he became aware of my interest in the outdoors and my desire to do some exploring, Huck invited me to come along on some excursions into the Ozarks. This included float stream trips, hiking, and what the formal world calls *spelunking*, but cavers just call caving.

Outdoor enthusiasts tend to aggregate, just like artists, musicians, politicians—no wait, let's not bring them into an otherwise pleasant discussion. In Columbia, Chouteau Grotto is a long-standing club devoted specifically to caving, but also to off-season trips to some lovely scenic spots in the quasi-wilds of Missouri. One might ask: Is there an off-season for caving? And yes, that would be mainly July and August, sweat, ticks, and rattlesnake season. So I gratefully accepted the invitation to join this group of adventurers, little knowing the wonders that were in store.

I could probably spend several pages just introducing the characters of my new friends, because that is what they all became. Cavers and outdoor folks come in many shapes and forms. There are as many professions, religions, shapes and sizes, and personalities represented as you could name, some with the desire to meet the challenges inherent in the rougher, dirtier outdoor sports, others not so much. But all these folks love the beauty and diversity of nature and will travel great distances and undergo considerable discomfort to experience it.

I hesitate to try to name everyone in the caving group for fear I will leave someone out. Kevin Feltz, Jim Huckins, Mac Johnson, Kay Stewart, Matt Gray, Scott Schulte, Randall Clark, Ron Kucera, Rick Walk, Jim and Bob Glock, Jim Ruth, Bob, Lillian, Annie, Joel, and others were all fixtures at the Crossroads West G&D Pizza and Steakhouse in Columbia on Wednesday night get-togethers. "Lots of beer in America!" However, some individuals played important roles in the stories so I'll include those, and ask forgiveness if I don't give everyone their moment of fame. So now we come to Brian Dollar, and since his stories are intertwined with some of these other friends, it will be their stories too.

When I first met Brian, it took me a while to figure out where he fit in my experiences. I finally decided he didn't. Aside from his unlikely Mennonite/Cherokee heritage, Brian is a unique and complex individual. Some stories of our shared experiences will bear that out. I don't recall how many trips we were on together before we really became acquainted, but we ended up doing quite a few excursions together, along with Huckins and others of the group.

Travels with Brian

While we were on a lot of caving trips together, not all my Brian stories involve caves. There was a memorable float on the Missouri River with Brian, Matt Gray, and my daughter Jennifer and her friend Jason (who were both about fifteen years old at the time). We camped on a gravel bar island, and oh, we also had some excellent brownies. I will just say that we had a groovy and memorable float and the scenery was great.

On another excursion Jenn, Jason, and I followed Brian on a hike that was supposed to end up at a destination but never did. If you've been around fifteen-year-olds you will no doubt appreciate that there was considerable criticism of his leadership skills and descriptive name calling. Brian took some mild exception to the term 'butt wipe,' stating that, okay, if he was Butt Wipe Number One, then they were Butt Wipe Number Two and Butt Wipe Number Three for following him. I said, "Leave me out of this 'Charmin' conversation."

On another occasion, Brian showed up at my place around nine o'clock one evening to invite me to help him locate a cave entrance somewhere in the Three Creeks area.

Now I know this sounds like a nefarious proposition but knowing Brian I knew it was an honest, if not reasonable, request, even though I had to be at my research assignment early the next morning. Eventually he wore me down and off we went. By the way, there were a couple of factors I should mention. First, there was an approaching storm. No problem, we would only be gone an hour or so. Second, I wasn't aware that Brian already had most of a twelve pack under his belt. Who knew? He never shows the effect of alcohol other than that he comes up with wild and crazy ideas; I should have known by now. As we were wandering around in the woods in the dark, thunder and lightning all around, we passed a tree I knew I had seen twice before already. "Brian," I said, "it's time to go home."

The last time he came by, several years later, it was around two in the morning. He woke me up with another invitation, this time to go 'mudding' at the new Big Muddy Wildlife Refuge. I firmly sent him home. Enough was enough.

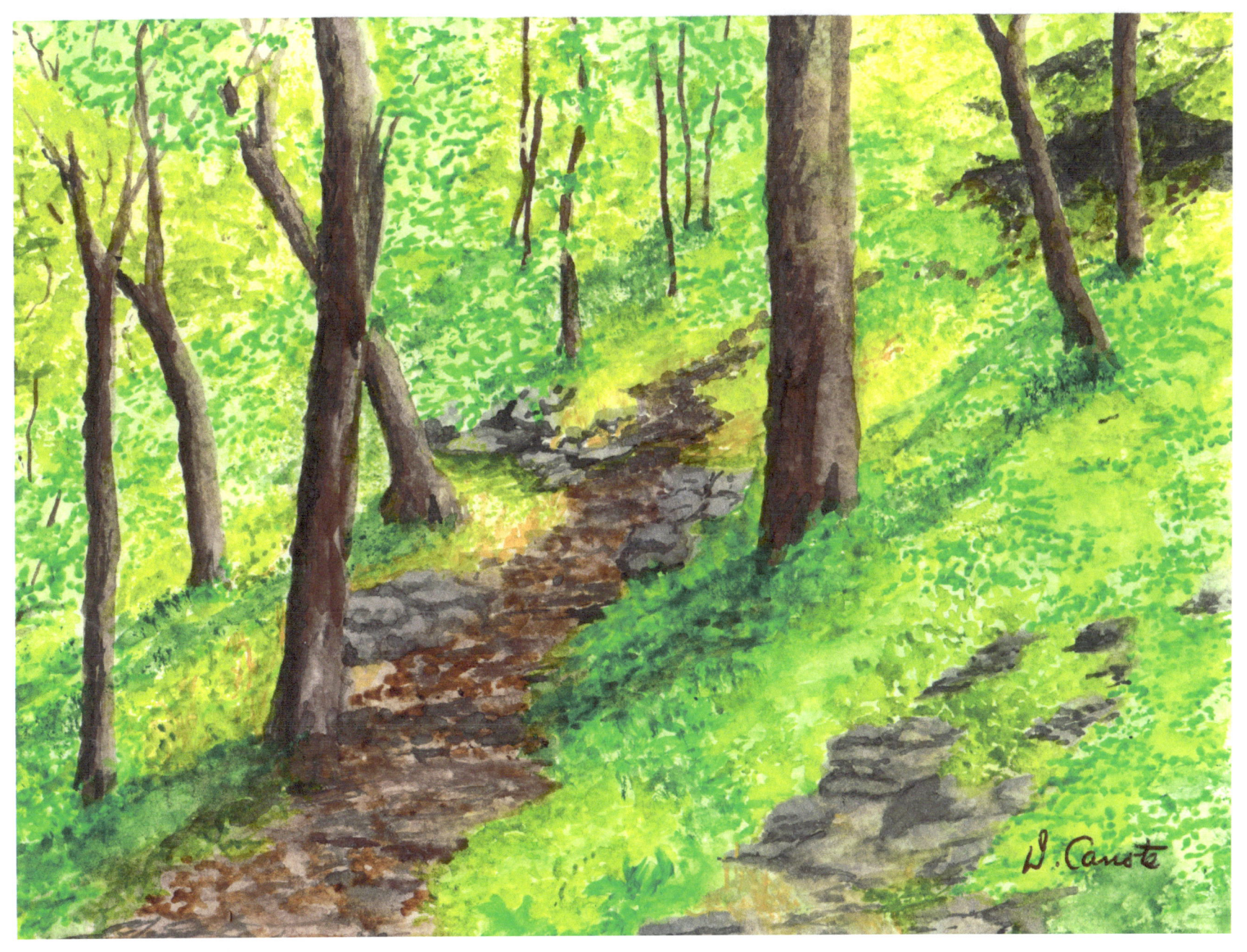

My Excursion into the World of Caving

Caves

A cave is a hole in the ground. It is dark, sometimes dry, sometimes wet, but nearly always a constant given temperature for any specific latitude. Some cave passages are broad and high, giving the impression of a cathedral, while others are serpentine labyrinths of crevices that lead up, down, branching and reconnecting. If the passages are wet and muddy it takes a die-hard sewer rat to enjoy them. Some are beautifully decorated with glistening features created by the dissolution and redeposition of minerals. Others are muddy, dirty, rocky and hell holes of misery.

As opposed to the touristy show caves that are lighted, guided, and even paved, wild caves are mostly difficult, challenging, hard to get to, and fragile in the sense that man-made damage cannot be repaired. In that sense, the location of these caves are often guarded by a closed-mouth attitude of preservation. They may house colonies of bats which are sensitive to disruption, especially during hibernation periods, or when they are carrying young. Other kinds of critters known only to specific caves are sometimes present, pale and reclusive as befits their habitat.

Caving as a Sport

There are two variations on caving. Horizontal caves are usually more or less just that, sometimes with one or more options as to exploring up and down sloping passages. Vertical caves are nearly always sinkholes, where underground passages collapse over time leaving a pit, with entry open to the air or by a short entrance. Many vertical caves may also have extensive horizontal passageways—a double whammy.

The closest activity to caving is rock climbing. However, lest you think for a minute that there is not much distinction between rock climbers and cavers, I'm going to make some broad generalizations about and comparisons between the two sports for those who do neither. There are some significant differences and I know what I write is not true in all instances. I can just hear some rock climbers blathering with a vehement rebuttal, but this is my opinion based on my observations and as they say, I'm stickin' to it.

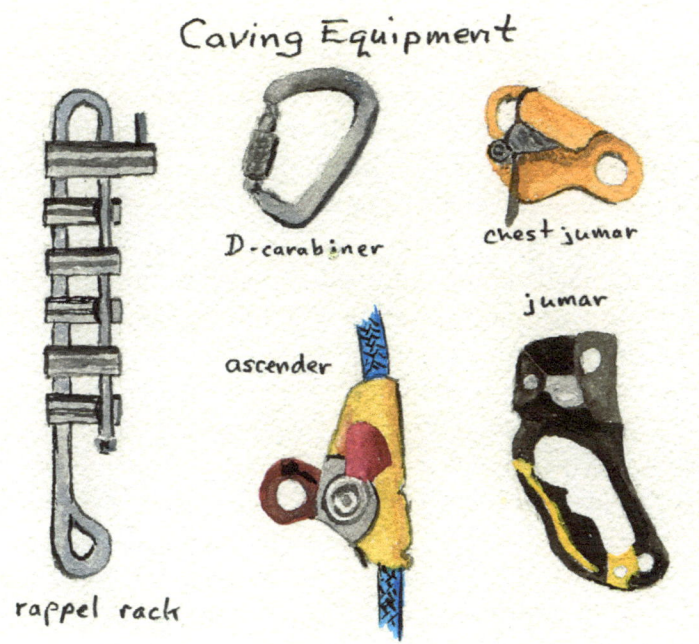

Caving Equipment

D-carabiner

chest jumar

jumar

ascender

rappel rack

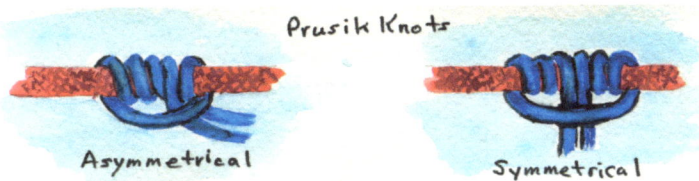

Prusik Knots

Asymmetrical

Symmetrical

Caving trips take quite a bit of preparation, especially for vertical caving (pits) and the amount of equipment and supplies can be considerable. Rock climbers outfit themselves with some *pitons* (rock spikes) and *carabiners* (oval or D-shaped links that can be opened and closed to attach the climber to the rope or equipment to the climber, a seat harness, and light *dynamic* (somewhat elastic) climbing rope, and resin for hand grip. Vertical cavers require a heavier, stiffer *static* rope which has less stretch, a hip and chest harness, and several metal devices in addition to the carabiners that attach to the rope to facilitate descent and ascent. Keep in mind that once you go **down** into the pit you still have to go back **up** to get out! The metal devices include; a ladder-like *rappel rack* about a foot long, through which the rope is threaded to control the rate of descent; steel carabiners; a *jumar* or other type of clamp that attaches to the rope and only allows movement in one direction—generally up; and aluminum *ascenders* that are fastened to the feet and legs in an ascent system called rope walking. In some cases climbers will use special ropes with *prusik* knots in place of the aluminum ascenders.

43

In addition to the equipment particular to this so-called sport, the clothing for caving is quite different from that of the rock climbers. A first necessity is a lighted helmet that uses either batteries or carbide. Extra of those power sources plus at least two other sources of light are standard. The attire of a rock climber consists of close-fitting shorts and shirts, often sleeveless, and special light-weight shoes designed to grip rock and resist slip. On the other hand, experienced cavers generally wear long pants, sturdy hiking boots with thick socks, and multiple layers of clothing depending on the time of year. Often the difference in temperature between above and below ground dictates addition or removal of layers for comfort. Caves average a constant temperature of around fifty-five degrees, depending on the amount of air movement and the presence or absence of water passage. Being cold and wet for an extended period of time can bring on hypothermia, so even though the exertion of walking, crawling, and climbing can work up a decent sweat, keeping warm during periods of inactivity such as resting, napping or, saints forbid, getting stuck or injured have to be considered. And in case you are wondering, in keeping with the caver's motto—take nothing out, leave nothing behind—that includes calls of nature.

Although rock climbers often travel great distances to do climbs, they are usually able to drive to their destination, hauling themselves and their equipment and supplies. They don't generally have to hike great distances through briar-, snake-, or tick-infested woods and ravines and rocky streams to get to their objective, carrying on their backs all the food, lights, ropes, cameras and whatever else they might conceivably need.

Rock climbing is usually done in good weather, in the open air. While that was never in my range of interest, I can see the attraction of challenging yourself physically and mentally, testing your endurance and mental toughness, and finally reaching a summit where you can see forever. Also, assents and descents can usually be planned in detail beforehand, taking some of the guesswork out of the process.

Finally, if you have done rock climbing or have even just stood by and watched the ascent, you can appreciate the physical and moral support of fellow climbers who stand by to belay the climber on rope and call out advice. "There's a hand hold up and to your left." "Move your right foot up, there's a rock you can rest on." "Atta boy, good job!" You get the idea.

With caves, on the other hand, you start out with one big question. Are you claustrophobic? Does the idea of having a mountain of rock above you make you wet your pants? Then just forget it, go sit under a tree. I have only once or twice had a claustrophobic experience in a cave, and that was brought on by a tight crawl space which briefly flashed back to getting stuck crawling under a porch as a kid. For those who have had that experience, you may recall that it comes on in an instant and you have an absolute blind terror and panic. Primal flight. Well, in a cave you can't give in to that. You have to get a good mental grip and as Bob Dylan's song says, "...give yourself a good talkin' to...."

Next, let me say that it is never a good idea to go into a cave alone. Even experienced cavers in good physical condition can have accidents. But even though you go in teams, situations may evolve so that your cohorts can't see you or don't know you're in trouble. Or if you are in trouble and they can't get to where you are, they can't tell you what to do because if they do yell out advice it echoes and you can't tell what the hell they are saying. So you have to be *very* vigilant, thinking always of the danger of injury or death and the burden of your rescue on your companions. And it can be a very lonesome and very scary proposition. You learn a lot about yourself in a cave.

And lastly, but by no means least, a cave can beat you up. By the time you have loaded yourself up with equipment (no sherpas here!), trekked up or down one or more Ozarky hills and hollers, crawled and chimneyed through horizontal and vertical crevices, water passages, over and between house-sized boulders, all in the presence of only a headlamp and one or more other crazy people, you will have burned all the calories you consumed at the last three meals and used every muscle of your aching body. If you are very lucky and careful, you will have only minor scrapes and bruises, but if you're not, they may have to haul you out like a sack of feed, which is totally humiliating.

I do have to admit that the above are worst case scenarios. The cavers who initiated me to the sport, especially Huck and Kevin, were the most careful, conscientious, and able instructors and mentors I could have hoped for. Their careful planning and attention to detail resulted in successful trips and safe returns home. The only troubles I had on these trips were entirely of my own making.

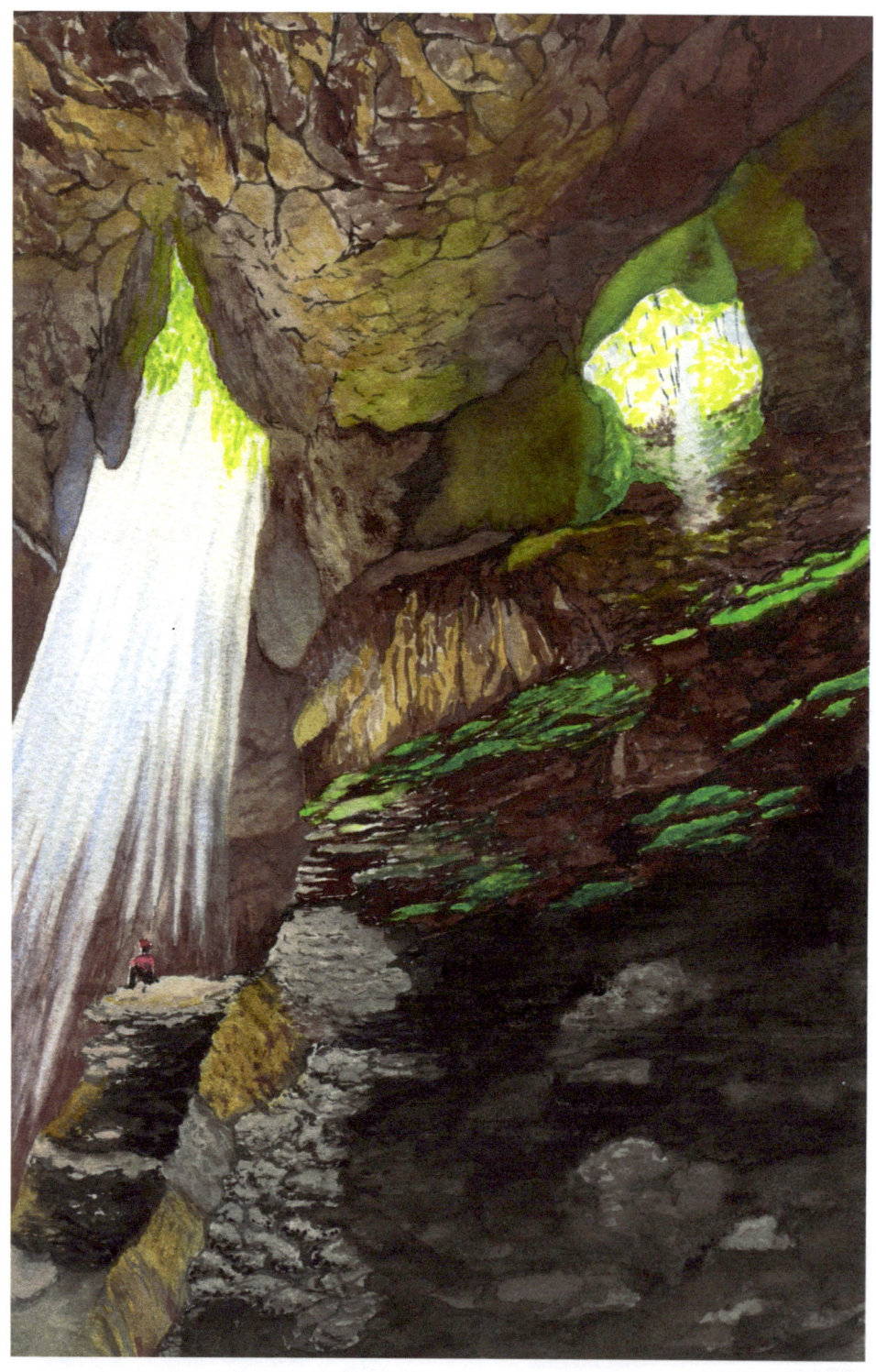

Glory Hole

Probably the most entertaining story involving Brian, Huck, and Kevin is of a caving trip to the area referred to as TAG, which is the area where the borders of Tennessee, Alabama, and Georgia abut. Like Missouri and other states with bedrock remnants of ancient seas, much of it is underlain with limestone and what is known as *karst* topography. Rainwater acidified by carbon dioxide infiltrates this stratified rock and over time dissolves its way through the strata until it is full of fissures and caves. Some are entered and explored through horizontal openings and tunnels at the ground's surface, while others are full of crevices and huge caverns that are accessible only by ropes and rappelling equipment. Many also are 'active' caves, still in the process of evolving and have streams, pools, and waterfalls that contribute to the challenge.

On this particular summer trip, Jim Huckins, Kevin Feltz, Brian, my daughter Jennifer, and I (and one or two other fellows whose names elude me), entered a stream passage near the top of a mountain, near a sign that said, "See Rock City," laden with a variety of ropes and paraphernalia necessary to experience this particular cave. Well, not by me, who decided to forgo the drop, or by Jenn, who at that time was only thirteen or so and had no experience on rope.

There was some waist- to chest-deep stream passage (fifty-five degree water) to reach a spot where a side branch of the stream had been partially blocked by a rock and mortar dam above an internal waterfall. Below the waterfall was another level of cave to be explored. The water was funneled through a short piece of drain pipe, about eighteen inches in diameter, which could be blocked to back up the stream flow into a pool and allow one to rappel down by rope to the lower level. After one or two persons had dropped, the block could be removed to empty the pool, then the process was repeated until all were down who were going. When they were ready to ascend, the process would be repeated in reverse (in theory) until everyone was out. Brian, Jenn, and I opted to stay in the stream passage above the waterfall and serve as the support group. Now to some of the interesting parts.

Item Number One: The Dam (Damned) Blockage.

Jim Huckins, brilliant scientist and self-taught engineer, rigged a piece of plywood board about twenty-four by thirty inches. Stapled to one side was a matching piece of closed-cell foam, to fit against the drain pipe to make a tight fit and allow the water to back up into the pool. To keep it dry, he covered this with a heavy-duty garbage bag, all tied and taped to hold it together. It was the job of Brian, Jennifer and myself to manipulate this blockage or plug in the afore-described manner so that everyone could do their upping and downing.

Item Number Two: Communication- Ho, Ho, Ho!

If you have ever been in a cave you will recall this; if you haven't you would need to know; caves echo. One cannot yell back and forth with any degree of certainty what the words are you are hearing. Also, two-way radios and the like do not work well in a cave due to the fact that radio waves don't travel well through or around rock. So, how to communicate between upstairs and downstairs when it is time to close the dam and let the folks downstairs come up? Someone came up with a system that would possibly work, namely that when they were ready to ascend, they would just let out a yell to get our attention and we would install the plug. After one or two and ascended, we would yell out, "Ho..., Ho..., Ho...!" (allowing a brief space between 'Ho's to account for the echo), following which we would open the dam and empty the pool. This way no one would be on rope when the waterfall came down. And now the issues.

Issue with Item Number One.

The main issue was the power and insidious nature of water. Despite the clever engineering, the garbage bag was not impermeable to water. As it seeped through the layers and tape and filled the bag, Huck's device began to fail, allowing an increasingly greater trickle of water to escape around the edges to the point that even the closed-cell foam began to come loose from the board. It worked fairly well initially.

The dam (damned) device was put in place prior to the descent of the lads down the 250-plus-foot drop to the lower chamber. The climbers got on rope and rappelled down, one at a time. After each descent the support team removed the dam and allowed the water to empty out of the pool. However, as the water rose in the pool, it became harder and harder to pull the plug, so to speak, and wrestling with this problem stressed the plug. With each removal and replacement the system continued to fail, and more and more water seeped out around the edges. The result was that on the final removal, the water, having so much force, sucked the garbage bag away and loosened the foam, making the seal ineffective. Brian and I were aware of this only after the others were already down, so there was no way to let them know the problem—unless they were smart enough to see a garbage bag laying down there and wonder where it came from.

Issue with Item Number Two.

Well, there really was no issue. It was the, "Oh, S – – t!" factor due to item number one that was the real problem. The fellows below spent a while doing whatever it was they did, before yelling up a "Ho, ... Ho, ... Ho!" to let us know to plug the dam. We did the best we could, but the flow of water around the plug was significant. Finally, after cursing and debating, they decided someone would ascend in the waterfall and find out what the hell we were doing! Kevin, brave stalwart soul, was the first to ascend, through a steady and unpleasant trickle of water. Because we had been concerned with the difficulty of removing the dam plug against the pressure of rising water, Brian and I decided we should empty the pool between each ascent to minimize the volume of down-flow of the waterfall.

As soon as Kevin made his ascent looking like a drowned rat and was off rope, we got ready to open the plug, and Brian yelled down, "Ho, ... Ho, ... Ho!" Now those who know Kevin know that he has a very calm demeanor and a quiet voice, and it takes a lot to get him ruffled. So when he suddenly turned to us, wide eyed and quite loudly and firmly said, "*Oh, no!*" we looked at him and he said, "Huck is on rope!"

Of course we didn't pull the plug at that point, but were later told that Huck, being midway up the ascent, had a come-to-Jesus moment when he envisioned the full force of the waterfall landing on him. We didn't ask and he didn't mention the condition of his underwear when he finally got to the top. Besides, we were busy dealing with getting our last colleagues out of the basement.

Needless to say, subsequent trips and events generally had at least one excuse to bring out the rallying cry, "Ho, ... Ho, ... Ho!" followed by considerable laughter by all but an embarrassed Brian, and a still traumatized Huck, who never really saw the humor in the situation.

Footnote on image: The painting of Stevens Gap Cave in northern Alabama that accompanies this essay is based on a photo taken by Jim Huckins, who kindly granted me permission for its use. Jim is an accomplished and prolific photographer, and is especially good at cave photography. Unlike open air photos, the light in caves has to be carefully managed to obtain the best results, and composition requires an experienced and artistic eye. There are not photos of a lot of caving trips because of the extra effort needed to add cameras and equipment in addition to the load already required.

War Eagle

There are several cave trips that were more memorable than others, and one or two that made me seriously question my sanity. One that comes to mind was an Arkansas cave called Beauty, but which our group referred to as Fitton's Cave for its owner, Marty Fitton. The features of this cave were a series of physical and mental challenges including: a water entrance (wading for the other folks, swimming for klutzy me when I fell in); huge rooms of breakdown piles of boulders (known also as climbing caves since the result of the breakdown is that the ceiling moves higher and higher) through which one had to crawl up and over, around, and under bus-sized boulders to get from one side of the room to the other (think Marine Corps boot camp); a mud-slime slide that required a hand-over-hand rope ascent and descent (I spent that part in a big room, waiting and near-hypothermic as a result of my swim, wrapped in a solar blanket in total blackness); and finally, over twelve hours after we entered, a chimney crawl up and out of the cave at the top of the mountain at midnight.

Like the pain of childbirth, the memory of that trip receded with time, and some years later I went again with Huck, Kevin, Steve Olson, and Henry Gilsdorf back to the TAG area for a descent into War Eagle. This pit is around 350 feet deep, and the drop is rigged over a large flowstone lip at the entrance. Flowstone is the result of mineral deposition from a stream over a long period of time. The same calcite and silicate minerals dissolved by the water are recrystallized into a beautiful, smooth dome-shaped slide.

In this cave, the lip is undercut so that once you have dropped over the edge, the rope lays tight against the rock and there is minimal abrasion. However, when you ascend to leave the pit, you have to push against the rock with one hand to get the rope away from the rock, while moving your chest ascender and leg attachments up the rope. That would not have been a problem except that Steve and I ascended tandem, me ahead, with his weight below. Did we think this out beforehand? I think not.

After rope-walking up the 350 feet, I was pooped, and try as I might I could not push the rope away from the rock to get myself up and over the lip. Did I mention I was experimenting with prusik knots? Connecting to legs, chest and seat harness, these knots have to be moved up the rope by hand with each step up. I don't know how long I spent fighting and cursing the rope, the rock, cavers, and caving in general, it seemed like hours but was probably much less.

Had it not been that Henry had gone up first we might still be hanging there. Eventually Henry let down an additional section of rope and Steve transferred his weight onto it and off the main rope, standing in a loop or 'pigtail' while I finally was able to move myself up and out. He also did a bit of cursing as he remained suspended in the pigtail above the 350-foot drop making derogatory remarks about a certain portion of my anatomy and my speed of progress. Well, he did have plenty of time and the perspective to observe my derrier but after all, part of it was his fault, and, well... shoot. End of story.

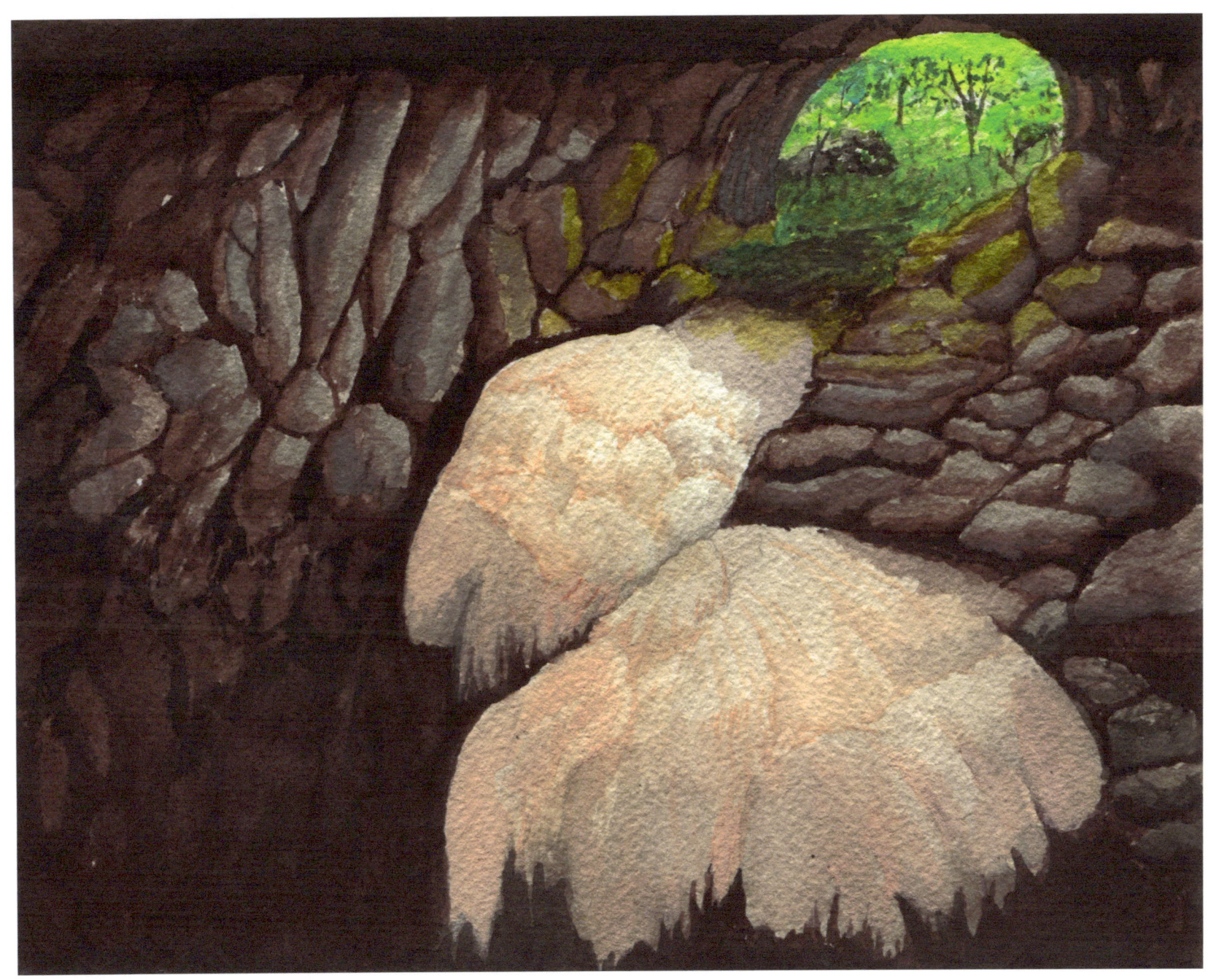

"But for now, this is one mighty fine mead hall, ain't it?

—Margaret Maron, *Death's Half Acre*

Chapter Four
Mexico: To the Border and Beyond

Travels to Mexico

Why Mexico? If you asked me in my younger years what part of the world I would like to visit, I might have said one of the European countries, as that is where my people came from. The British Isles, especially Ireland and Scotland, have always held a mystique for me. The Mediterranean coasts would also be attractive, but I probably wouldn't have thought of Mexico. Actually, I didn't really choose Mexico, initially grad studies took me there, and that started another affair—with Mexico.

Our family was, and still is, not particularly affluent, and as a result, we didn't do much traveling. My parents and the members of their generation were people of modest income, mainly working people. Some held jobs of public service, others were farmers, and a few were professionals with their own businesses. Those of my generation, myself, siblings, and cousins went further afield, as teachers, working for airlines, or working for the government, some traveling overseas and to various countries. To the best of my knowledge, most of us have led comfortable lives while contributing positively to society.

Two of the things necessary to travel are sufficient income and the time to spend it. My life was filled with the business of education, work, and family, none of which provided enough of either time or funds to do more. However, when I hit graduate school I literally and figuratively hit the road.

As a grad student and then a professional working in the sciences—agronomy, fisheries and wildlife, and contract toxicology—one goes where the research leads, which for me included various locations within the continental United States. Some of the travel was for field work, some for meetings, and all of this was my introduction to a world outside my previous experience.

But most interesting and fun was time and travel with the friends I made both inside and outside of the context of work. Many of these folks also worked in areas in or peripheral to the sciences, as researchers or environmentalists, and were already avid outdoors people. Travels canoeing, hiking, and caving eventually led me to Mexico. Especially after several trips to the southwest, it was inevitable I would go into that country.

Seminars in Tropical Ecology

It was difficult to decide whether to tell my stories chronologically or moving back and forth in time. I suppose the most logical is to introduce you to Mexico as I experienced it my first visit. The story isn't particularly thrilling, but the trip did have its moments.

I will jump back a bit to my graduate school era to explain why I went on that first trip. Like Sherlock Holmes, I was somewhat eclectic in selecting my course work. The courses in support of one's research and dissertation are naturally supposed to be relevant to the research and the field of study. I have to admit that I snuck in one or two that were either non-relevant or at best borderline. The one I reference here, *Seminars in Tropical Ecology*, was taught by Dr. John Faborg in the University of Missouri's Biology Department. The course required a week-long trip to Mexico over winter break; and who knew, it might be useful if I decided to go practice agronomy in Mexico, right? Right.

While I didn't take a camera along on the trip, I have several images indelibly fixed in my mind. One of these was of the sugarcane fields we drove by and through on our way to our field site. When you think of sugarcane, you may have a mental image of a stick filled with sugar. The plant itself resembles corn. In fact, it is a close relative of corn and sorghum, in the grass tribe Andropogoneae.

Growing to a height of up to twenty feet, it stores sucrose (sugar) in the cane stem. When it is ready to harvest, the fields are burned to remove the 'trash', making it easier to cut the cane. This is normally done by workers wielding machetes, as most of the fields are only five to ten acres, making the use of large equipment impractical.

Since our trip emphasized tropical ecology, I think it is worth saying something about the ecological impact of this crop's production. The obvious one is the increase in carbon dioxide release as a result of burning at a time when we recognize that we need to be reducing the carbon footprint in the atmosphere. Processing the cane to extract sugar also produces a lot of waste which requires disposal and which contributes to pollution of surface and ground waters. There is also adverse impact on the workers who harvest, due to smoke inhalation over long periods, as well as kidney damage due to dehydration in the fields.

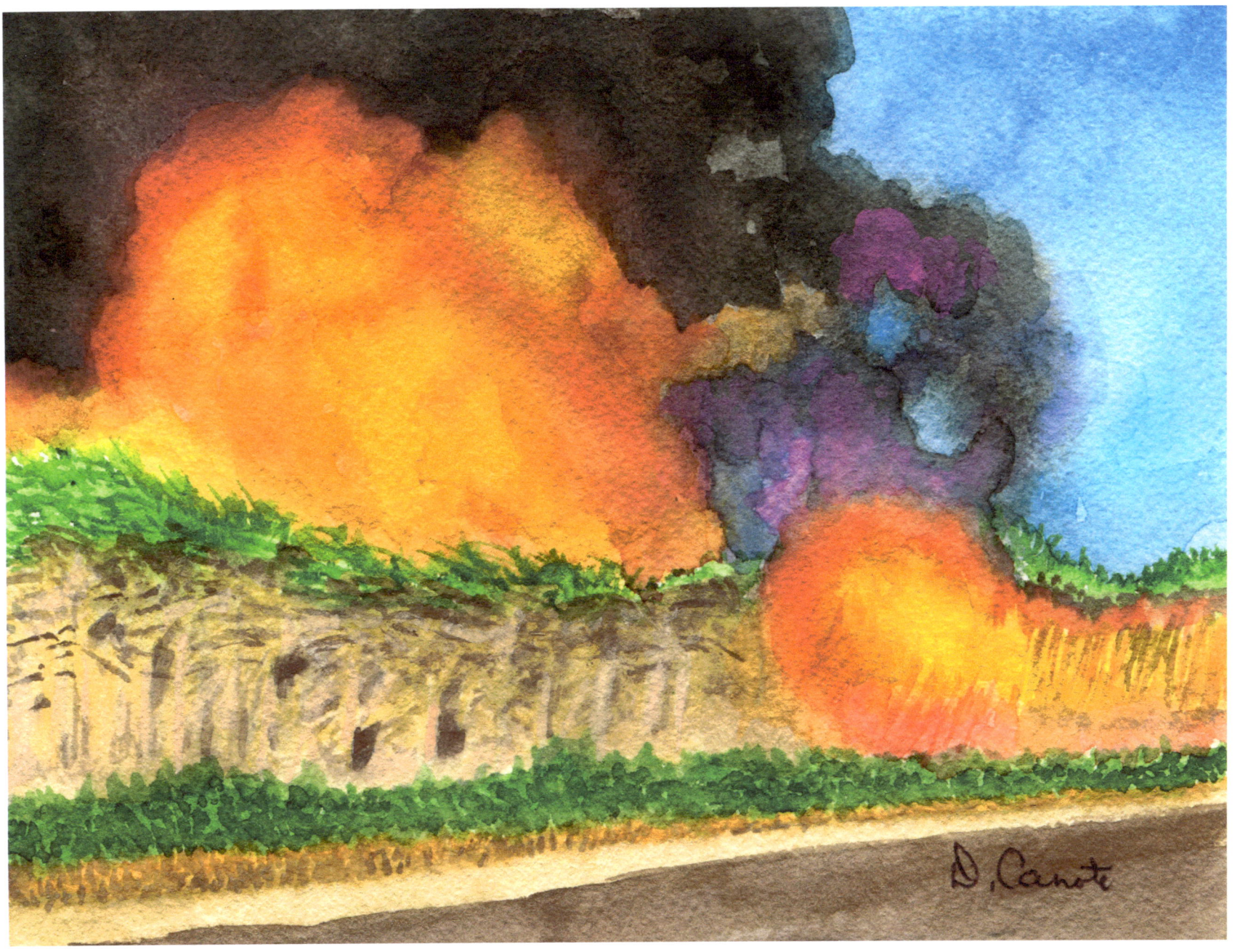

And now the rest of the story

I had never been out of the country and had no passport, but at that time you didn't need one to cross the border as long as you had a copy of your birth certificate and a voter registration card for your county of residence. I was thoroughly excited and spent hours packing, deciding what to take and what to leave home. In the end I managed to pare it down to a manageable backpack and bedroll, including a couple of Ziplock bags of my favorite homemade Tollhouse chocolate chip cookies to share.

There were about a dozen grad students and several other supervisors on the trip. Dr. Faborg, being in charge of the group, gave us an indoctrination and pep talk before we left. One item on his list was protocol for the border crossing. When we passed through customs and were asked for our home location we were to give our state of residence, but not necessarily the city. This was important because at least one of our group was from Mexico, Missouri. Needless to say, when her time came, the lass botched it and said exactly what she shouldn't. That was the first straw for the proverbial camel. We spent what seemed like ***hours*** in customs, and Dr. Faborg had to do all the explaining and perhaps financially lubricating the passageway of our group across the border. Good thing we had cookies to snack on.

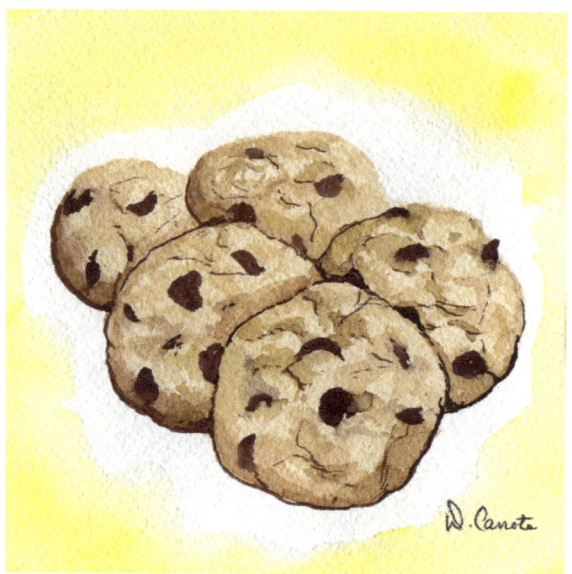

Whew. That accomplished, we continued south to our field study area in the Sierra Madre Orientales—the eastern range of those mountains. The location was a ranch owned by a lady named Juanita, a common destination for many United States–based university research groups. We camped out near a stream in a mountainous region and set up our tents, cooking area, and so forth. Sleeping arrangements involved sharing a tent with another student (same sex, of course), and while I didn't know my tent mate we seemed to hit it off well enough. Also, the chocolate chip cookies were a hit, although I had to spend considerable effort keeping them from being tossed around, sat on, or otherwise turned into crumbs as they passed back and forth.

The first night we were awakened in the wee hours by an eerie hissing scream that repeated itself several times. Having been warned not to stray from the camp area due to reports of jaguar sightings in the area, we lay wide awake for the rest of the night, speculating anxiously about the sounds, with visions of the tent being ripped open and one of us carried off as food. I don't clearly recall the details, but I think we were much better acquainted tent mates thereafter. By the way, when we asked the next morning if others heard the sounds, Dr. Faborg informed us it was the call of a barn owl. We looked at each other and shared a weak laugh, but thereafter we slept pretty soundly.

We were also warned about the hazards of the water supply in Mexico, including the use of ice in beverages. At that time bottled water was not a common commodity and one generally carried a supply of milk jugs or other containers for drinking, cooking, etc. I never gave it a thought the first morning as I went to the nearby stream after breakfast to brush my teeth. As I was brushing away, I looked up to see, upstream from our camp, a man with a small herd of cows he had brought to water. They were drinking and doing what cows do, and I thought, "Au Oh..." as I envisioned the rest of the trip either puking and/or with my pants around my ankles using up our meager supply of toilet paper.

Well thank God for small and great favors, because it didn't happen. A fellow caver commented on this when I related the story later, asking if I had cistern water to drink when I was younger. I recalled the ground wells at my home and my grandparents house, never treated as they are now with anti-everything, and began to better appreciate my country raising.

There were several other occurrences during our trip that tested the patience of our fearless leader, none particularly serious, but all additional straws on the load. At one point we had been let loose in some city market to go shopping with instructions to be back at the bus at a specific hour in order to make it to wherever we were bound next. At the appointed hour a couple of folks hadn't returned, so we waited with increasing anxiety on the part of Dr. Faborg as he no doubt envisioned further encounters with the Mexican officials, calls to parents, etcetera. Meanwhile, I passed out cookies to keep everyone's strength and spirits up.

It turned out to be just a case of lizard-brained incompetence on the part of the guilty parties, who lost track of time or came up with some lame excuse. Dr. Faborg was obviously pissed, and after a trip to the back of the bus to read them the riot act he returned to the front seat where, finding the bag of remaining cookies he stood up, turned around, and proceeded to thoroughly and dramatically mash the remaining cookies between his hands before handing me back the bag. Then he sat down and calmly instructed the bus driver to drive on.

Thus ended the first of my adventures in Mexico. I learned a lot, and not all of it was about tropical ecology.

Stories About My Truck

For our Big Bend float and for my second and third trips into Mexico we took my pickup truck which I rigged for carrying supplies and equipment. At this point in my story I think it worth telling you a bit about this wonderful truck. It was my first pickup, which I bought new, and some the guys at the lab where I was working made the snide comment, "What does she need a pickup for?" When I heard about this, I was sort of insulted and thought, "None of your gosh-darned business!" I probably used much stronger language. The truth was, I wanted the ability to haul people and stuff all over the place on these trips that had become part of my lifestyle. So there.

It turned out that this nifty vehicle played a big part in my life, partly because of what it allowed me to do and partly because of the way it changed how I saw and thought of myself. It was a blue 1988 Dodge Dakota long-bed, no extended cab, so I located an old aluminum camper shell the right length, set in on a one-by-four inch baseboard on front and sides, and covered the bed with a piece of five-eighths inch plywood with cutouts for the wheel wells. It had front and side windows, so I matched up the sliding passenger window in the Dakota with a cutout in the camper window and rigged a passageway between the two so I could access the front from the back and vise versa. This was essential for communicating with passengers in the back, since only two or three could fit comfortably in the cab.

Since I was going on quite a few float trips in those years, I built a rack on top using two-by-fours to carry one or two canoes. You've probably seen these jerry-rigged outfits going down the road carrying ladders, piping, and so forth, but I wasn't then and am still not particularly worried about what other people think about my ideas. I love doing carpenter work and I thought I did a bang-up job!

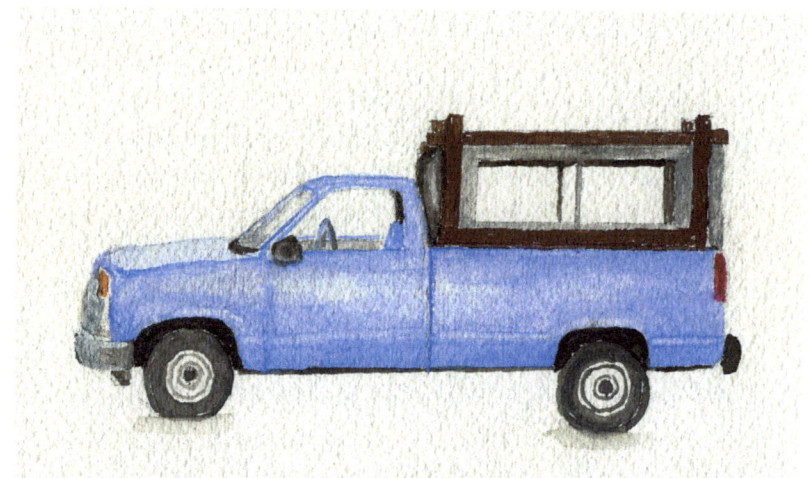

There was only one problem I ever had with the canoe rack, and that leads to another short story you may find amusing. A colleague at work, Jane Bowman, and I had to go to Houston, Texas for a meeting of some sort and she wanted to stop off along the way to visit her friend who was also her ex-husband. To save money and the hassle of airports I offered to drive my pickup. It's a long way to Houston so we decided to camp along the way. Both of us being outdoor girls, we weren't much concerned with roughing it a bit, so we pulled into Quanah Parker State Park midway between Dallas and Houston. (This was where I encountered the asp!). It's an interesting place to visit, with a historic fort and an interesting history. If you have never heard of Quanah Parker, a Comanche war leader, you might like to look him up. As an interesting side note, I later met a great grandson of Quanah Parker—big guy, really nice—while working on a wood canoe with environmentalist and newspaper columnist, Ken Midkiff in Columbia, Missouri.

Later that evening, as we were trying to sleep in the back of the truck, we had a visit from some raccoons trying to have their own picnic from the coolers we left on the picnic table. Don't recall how we dealt with that, it wasn't traumatic.

A final story on the Houston leg of that trip is about pulling into the parking garage of our hotel. I had paid no attention to the clearance signs and didn't even know how tall the canoe racks were, so as we pulled in slowly, looking for a parking space, we were brought to an abrupt halt, and the truck refused to move forward. I got out and looked and, sure enough, not enough clearance. What to do? The vertical supports of the rack were higher than the horizontal boards, so I thought, why not remove that part? I had once been accused by a friend who said that, like him, I carried around a subset of all my belongings in my vehicle. And sure enough, I had my toolbox in the back with a 'short cut' saw, so I cut those suckers off! I'm sure those city folks using the garage would have been amused had they driven in and watched the process, but hey! Problem solved. We proceed to park and check in without further incidents.

When it became obvious that I needed more cargo capacity for Mexico trips, I installed a floor that rested on support legs and the wheel wells, with the middle back cut in two sections and each section hinged to allow access to the underneath. That way you could lift up either or both sides to store equipment over the whole truck bed area and still have plenty of room to sit up comfortably on the newly constructed floor. Pretty slick. And you could also lie down and take a nap or bunk for the night. Driving south, two of us would ride in the back and then switch places so no one had to suffer too much from a numb behind.

I had my truck until 2001. It took me on a lot of trips to Texas to visit friends and family, and on lots of vacations, as well as back and forth to work. Eventually it started to develop glitches as aging vehicles often do, dying and stranding me at stop signs and parking lots, until my mechanic neighbor, Mark Santora, finally 'easter-egged' it into revealing a faulty electronic part. In the end, I sold it to a young ex-Amish fellow who was willing to take a chance on it, and we still saw it going up and down Boone County roads for a number of years thereafter.

On the Border with Mi Amigos
Floating the Rio Grande

Christmas break most years were an excuse to leave the misery of a Missouri winter and head south for some outdoor adventure. One year I was coerced into joining Brian Dollar, Steve Olson, and Kay Stuart into a trip to Big Bend to float a section of the Rio Grande through Santa Elena Canyon. Steve, Brian, and Kay drove down together a day before I could get away, so it was just me and my trusty Dodge Dakota heading out early one morning for Texas. You might bear in mind that this was the mid-1980s, before cell phones were a common appendage of everyone and their dogs. The Internet was also in its early days and a lot of information was not then at my fingertips. Knowing what I know now, I might have done things differently.

It takes a long time to drive from Columbia, Missouri to the southern border. I don't recall when I left home, but I made it to Marathon, Texas sometime in the evening hours. The only open and obvious place I found with rooms was the prestigious Gage Hotel, which was way above my grad student budget. Upon inquiring as to parks in the area where I might park and camp overnight, the hotel clerk, with a somewhat dubious expression, suggest a city park about ten minutes south. He didn't say that ten minutes south was actually five miles out of town (it's a pretty small town).

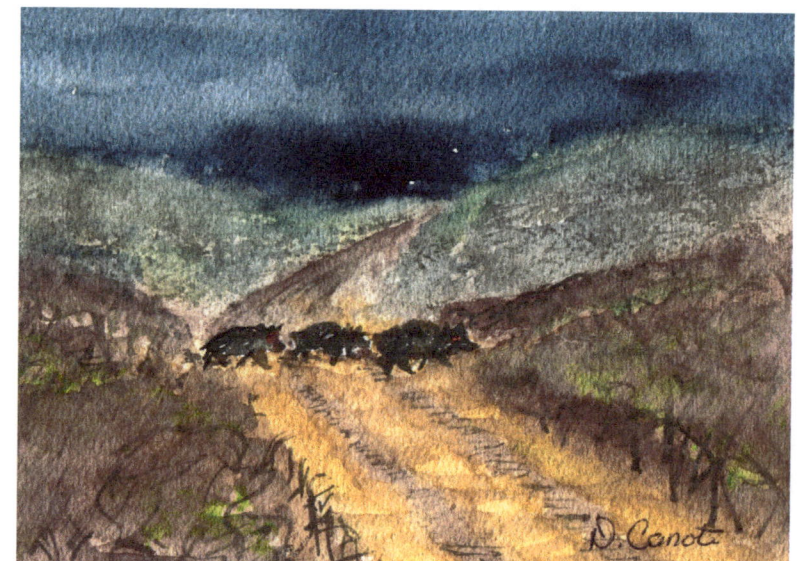

So I headed south, and as I drove I noted no houses or ranches, no other roads, lights, no *nada* as far as I could tell. Driving cautiously, I had almost reached the park when I saw movement off to my left in the brush. Ahead, in the low-water crossing, a small group of critters appeared in the headlights as they passed in front of the truck—javalenas! Whoa! No tent camping for me that night!

The park had a small maintenance building, a few picnic tables, and not much else as far as I could tell from the headlights of the truck. I parked near the building and crawled in the back of my truck camper shell with my sleeping bag and tried to get comfortable. I was just about asleep when I heard another vehicle pull into the park. Looking out I saw several people getting out and began to seriously rethink my situation. It dawned on me that nobody—***nobody!***—knew where I was. All the suspense novels I was so fond of provided a variety of scenarios as to what might unfold from that point. I hunkered down, pulled the sleeping bag up over my head, and did the obvious thing—I prayed. I guess it worked, because after about an hour the party broke up and everything was quiet for the rest of the night.

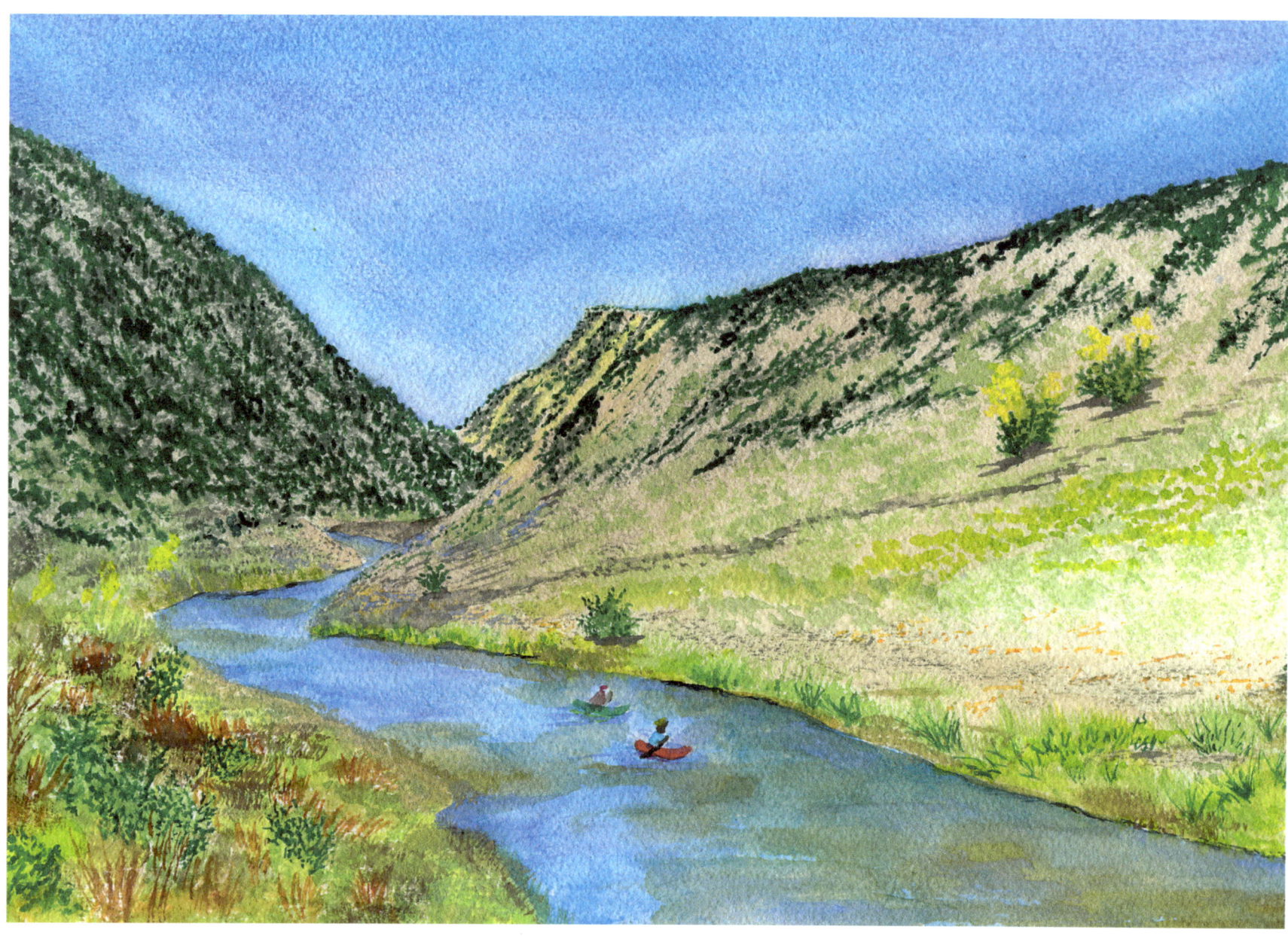

I experienced something else on that trip that I have never experienced before or since—I was convinced I was going to drown in the waters of the Rio Grande. A heavy weight of foreboding settled on my mind as I drove south from Marathon to the point where we had planned to meet. We camped near Terlingua, an old silver mining town, over New Year's Eve and went to the local cantina for some beers and local wildlife. I won't detail the rest of that evening, but sum it up by saying it was revealing and memorable. My readers are free to ask me about it some time.

The next day we packed up and headed for our put-in at Lajitas. By evening we had completed our shuttle. I don't need to detail all the back and forth driving that is required to shuttle vehicles from take-out to put-in on a river float. If you've done it you know how boring it is; if you haven't, trust me, it's boring.

As evening approached, Brian, Kay, and I were at the put-in waiting for Steve to drive back from shuttling, when Brian made the executive decision that he and Kay would put in and float ahead of us to find a camping place before dark. I had visions of Steve and I starting out alone after dark and floating on unknown waters looking for the camp and wasn't thrilled at being left at a border crossing alone with the canoe and camp gear. You might recall my premonition. . . . When Steve finally returned, it was nearly dark and upon learning of the situation he proceeded to have a major melt down, throwing gear out of the truck and vowing to leave it all—and me!—and go home. Whoa. Talk about a sphincter-puckering situation. Details of the ensuing discussion are omitted here, but eventually sanity was restored, we put in, floated on, and found the others at a camp site.

From there, the float was mainly uneventful. Santa Elena canyon was beautiful, the water at a level that enabled us to avoid boulders and other hazards and obstacles until we got to our next camp site. We did dump once, thanks to my forgetting that when you want to avoid overhead tree branches you need to *lean downstream!* The water was shallow and we managed to recover most, if not all, of the canoe's contents. However, I don't recommend the water of the Rio Grande for drinking. As I pulled myself onto the bank, I looked down and noted the deposits on the rocks, I was reminded of the dried manure from cow pies of Missouri farms. I decided it didn't make any difference, because— Ha!—I was going to die anyway.

That night, having set up camp again in a relatively low-relief area, we wrangled up some chow. (Isn't that what you say on the frontier?) We were sitting around rehashing the day's events when we noted some riders with pack burros crossing the river upstream of our camp one or two at a time and heading north. Naturally, Brian and Steve were like guard dogs on alert, and spent some time speculating on what they might be doing. Smuggling dope? Planning to rob or kidnap some gringos? We watched for an hour or so as the riders passed on into the adjacent hills and canyons to the north, occasional flashes of light indicating their path. Eventually, Kay and I left them to their watchdogging, crawled into our tents, and proceeded to go to sleep. At this point I could care less, because... *you know.*

The end of this story is anticlimactic. I didn't die, nothing else exciting happened, we made it through Santa Elena Canyon, got to our take-out and did the last shuttle to retrieve Steve's truck, and headed back home. Later I did some research on the matter of smuggling and discovered that there was a brisk business in wax from the candelilla plant. Now that was a revelation.

Teaching Moment: The Candelilla Plant

Yes, it's that time again, school is back in session. There is so much about our country and its history that we never hear about, so every time I happen on one of these obscure topics I have a need to, like a woodpecker on a dead tree, winkle out the juicy stuff hiding in the cracks.

Euphorbia antisyphilitica, aka 'wax plant,' is a tufted perennial native to the trans-Pecos region of Mexico and the southern U.S. It has been commercially important since the early nineteen hundreds as its waterproof coating is the source of a high grade wax used in making candles, soap, ointments, sealing wax, phonograph records, insulation material, shoe polish, floor polish, waterproofing, and lubricants. South of the border its production is subsidized and controlled by the Mexican government, but it seems to be more profitable for harvesters to bring the plants into the U.S. to sell to processors here. It is not an illegal import and there are still a number of wax processing plants operating in Texas.

If you are interested in learning more, you can find an extensive and thorough history of the topic of the wax plant on the *Texas—Beyond History* website. For myself, the attraction is in the quality of the candles produced from the wax of this plant. The color of the candles is a golden brown, and the light produced has a warm beauty that has no doubt long shed its glow into the homes and churches of the people of Mexico. I still have some I brought home from my trips south of the border, and am waiting for a particularly meaningful evening to light them. Or maybe when I pass over the border of my life, my family and friends will light them and think warm, happy thoughts of me.

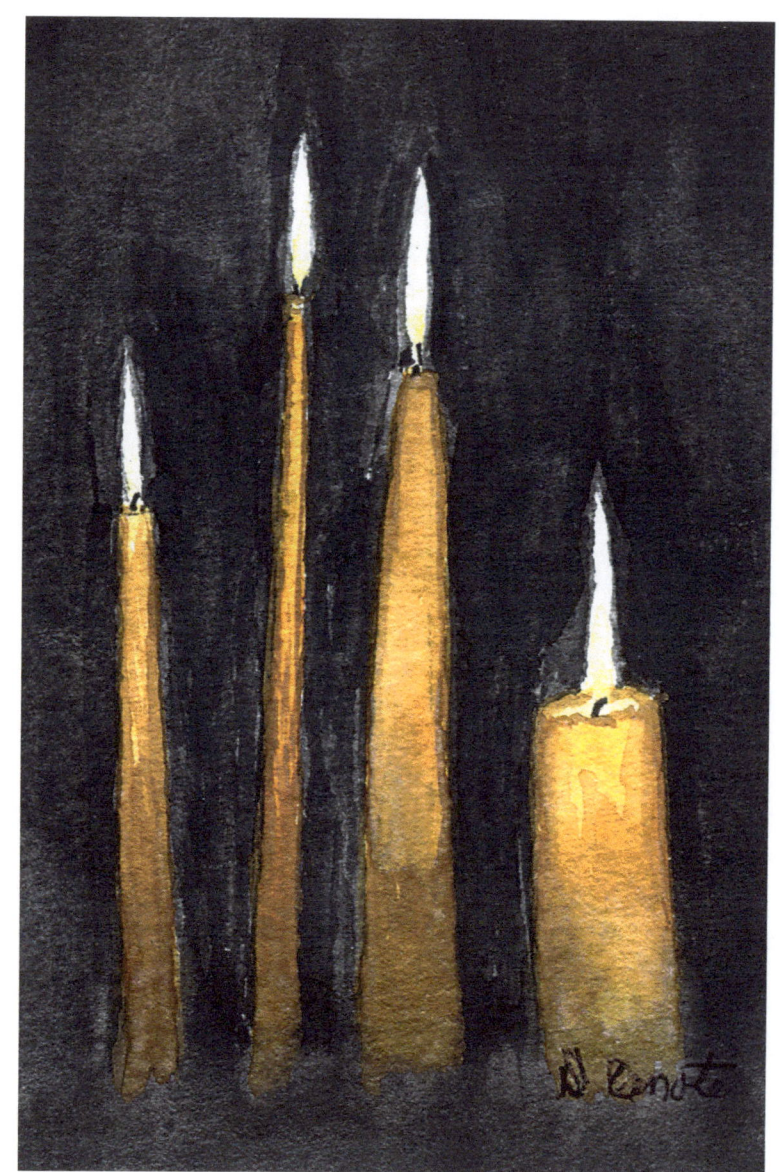

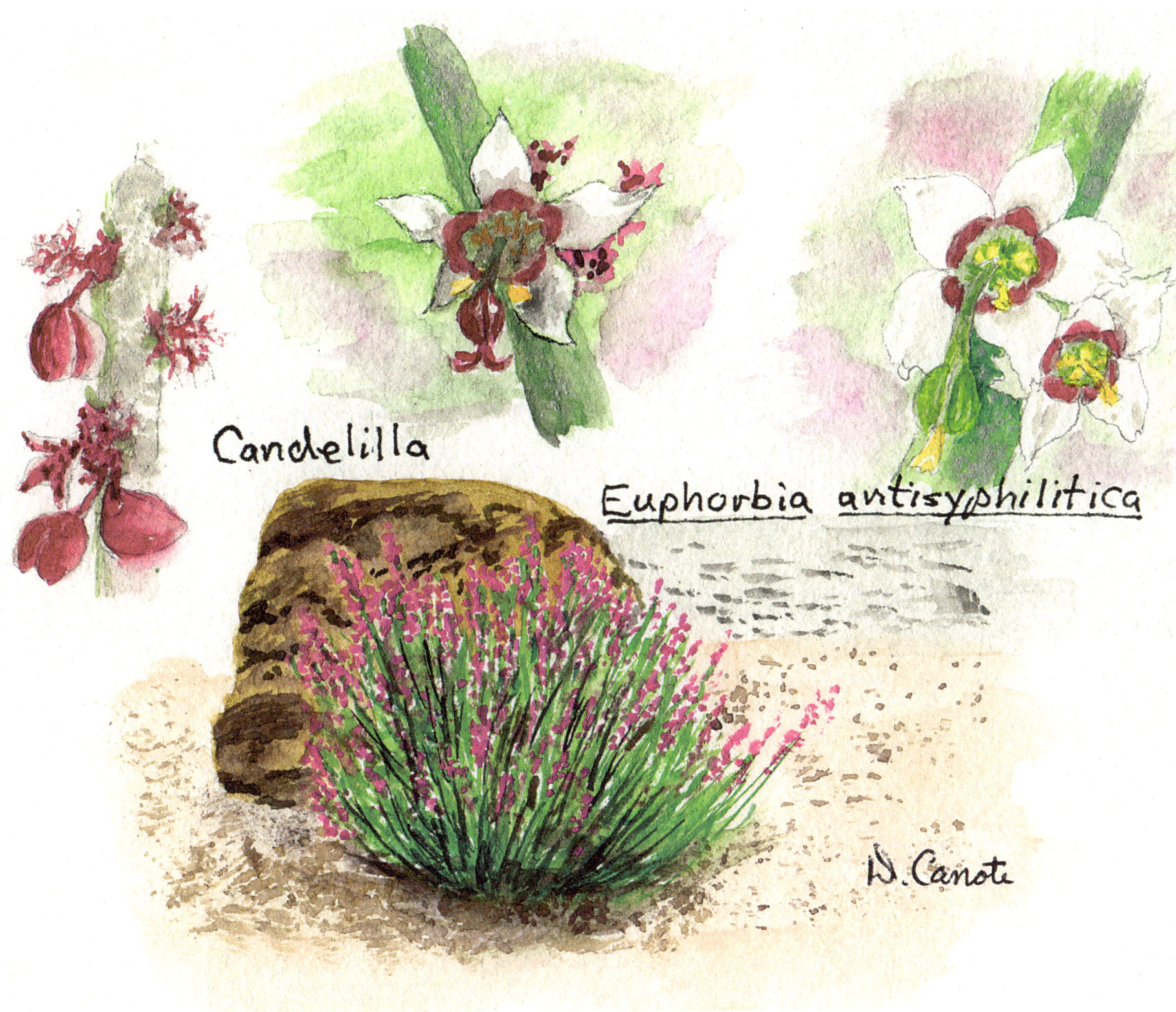

Candelilla

Euphorbia antisyphilitica

D. Canote

Into the Eastern Mountains

Getting into the Country

The mountain system in Mexico consists of three main ranges—the Sierra Madre Oriental to the east, the Sierra Madre Occidental to the west, and the southern Sierra Madre del Sur, which together enclose the great central Mexican plateau. The first three trips I went on were into the eastern range of the Sierra Madres. The eastern mountains, like many in the central and eastern United States, are of sedimentary origins with corresponding patterns of weathering forming karst topography, i.e. caves. However, as a result of its warmer, more tropical weather the cave systems of Mexico have developed on a much grander scale, producing enormous sinkholes and deep systems of caverns. Many of these are water-filled and a destination for international cave divers.

My first Mexico trip with my caving friends was initially more of a tourist trip, in that there was as much sight-seeing as caving. Steve Olson, Brian Dollar, my daughter Jennifer, and I set out at the start of winter break, crossing the border at Laredo, Texas. Getting through customs was much easier then, except for one custom—the *mordido* (the bite).

Most everything that involved any level of bureaucracy in Mexico was expedited by a few *dineros*. When the border agent, who seemed to be less than proficient in English, promised a "special service," adding, "It's up to you," we all looked at each other and thought, "What?" None of use knew much of any *Español*, and started a dialog... What is he saying? What does he want? Acting about as dumb as he obviously thought we were. After five or ten minutes of looking puzzled, shrugging our shoulders, he evidently decided the stupid gringos were more trouble than the effort required. Plus, we didn't really have any dineros to spare, and we did look pretty disreputable. So he basically said, "Get the heck out of here," and let us go. Whew.

Our first marathon drive day took us as far as Monterrey, Mexico. We stopped at a McDonald's for dinner, which was a revelation of modern construction, with a huge atrium and two levels connected by a broad, gleaming staircase bannistered in chrome and metallic gold rails. Couples were dressed in brilliant white shirts and blouses and stylish dressy shoes and suits as they would dress to go to a night club. I fear our trip-weary grunge didn't do much to impress the locals, and we took our food to go.

We found a modest motel to spend the night. Brian at that time had a major problem with a foot fungus, so we made him leave his socks and boots outside the door. The next morning his socks were missing (thankfully the boots weren't). We enjoyed a good laugh at his expense and blamed the theft on the ubiquitous dogs so common in the area.

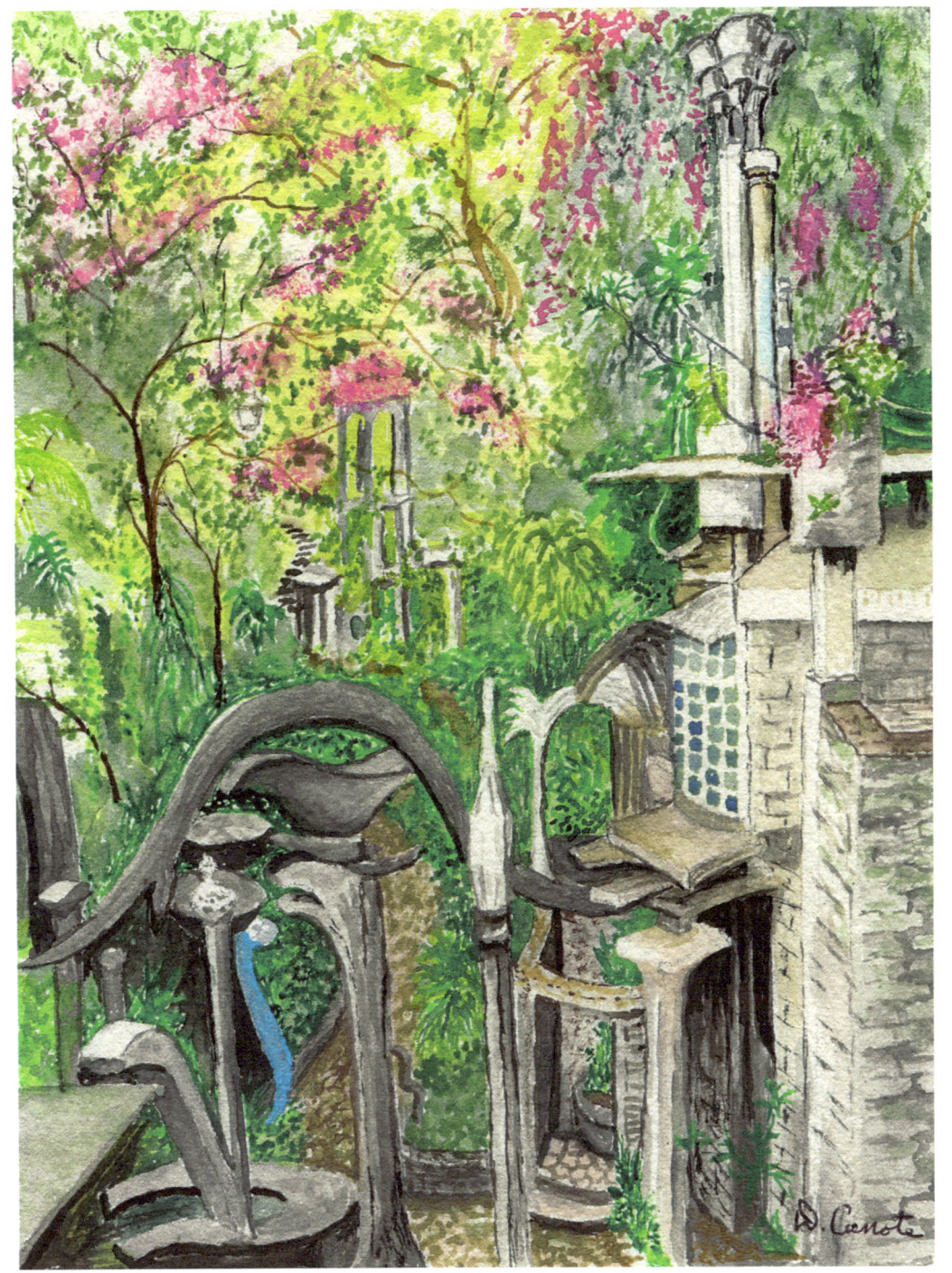

Driving farther south to the state of San Luis Potosi, we were in search of the town of Xilitla, where we hoped to see a site known as Las Pozas. In 1947 Edward James, English poet, artist, and patron of the surrealist movement, acquired a coffee plantation near Xilitla which he used as a location to establish exotic animals and plants. In 1962 he initiated the construction of an exotic sculpture garden. At the time of his death in 1984 the gardens consisted of thirty-six surrealist sculptures covering over forty acres. We slept at the gates of the site and spent most of the next day exploring the garden, which consisted of winding paths through a bizarre landscape of open-roofed rooms, pools, and stand-alone pedestal stairs extending into the air to … nowhere! Word had it that the bare re-bar extending from the ends of some of the concrete objects indicated that the construction was unfinished, which meant no taxes were yet due. Pretty clever.

Moving on from Xilitla, we headed to a sort of ritzy (for us) resort hotel out in the country called Hotel Taninul. The hotel staff were a bit hesitant to rent us rooms, grungy and rough as we looked, but eventually we got settled in. One of the main attractions there is a quite large swimming pool fed by mineral hot springs. Just so you know, this sort of pool is also a favorite of some sort of algae that tends to coat the bottom and sides, and presumably loves sulfur, because the water is pretty fragrant with its smell. One night there, and then on to the final destination.

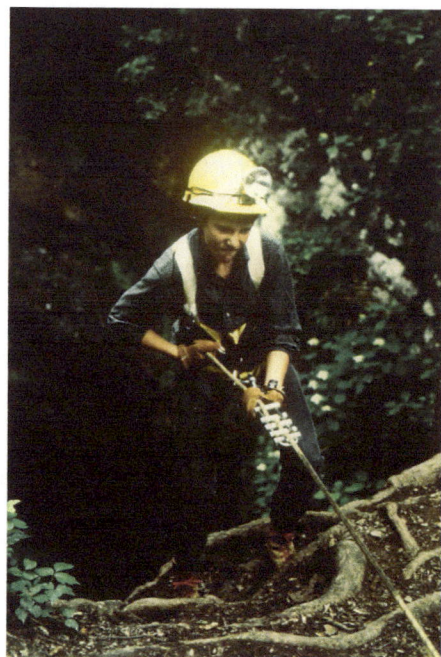

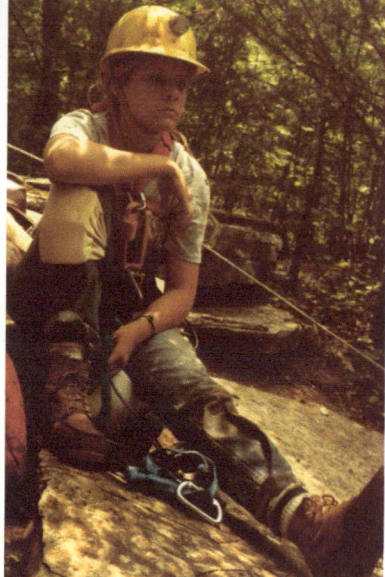

Guaguas

Hoya de las Guaguas (pronounced *wá wus*) is a giant sinkhole cave. Roughly translated, this is the pit of either the babies or the bus. I'm not sure whether this is because the opening is big enough to throw in a bus, or it was the site where the natives once sacrificed babies. Probably best not to think about it.

Located near Xilitla, the pit has a total depth of nearly fifteen hundred feet. A caving friend, Henry Gilsdorf, along with another caver met us at the foot of the mountain with a the rope for the descent. Henry and the others carried the rope up the rugged climb to the mouth of the pit, and let me just say that fifteen hundred feet of rope weighs enough that most people hire a burro for the job. Henry did it mostly by himself. He's not a big guy but his strength was awesome!

Because the depth was so great, the time for the descent and the climb out of the cave precluded all of us being able to do it. Henry, his friend, and Steve planned to go down and Jennifer, who had been doing rope work and was fit and active, wanted to go. Steve and Henry agreed to help her *in loco parentis* while Brian and I stayed topside to look after the equipment and make sure no one untied the rope. Ha ha. We were nobody's fools.

Well, we had a long wait, and were kept company by a Mexican lad of about six, who fell in thrall of my hand-carved walking stick. Made by an artist friend, it was topped by the face of an old bearded man with a floppy top hat. The boy sat with us and talked to the stick, trying his best to make me understand that he badly wanted to keep it. I felt bad disappointing him but it also meant a lot to me, and he finally gave up and went home.

Eventually the climbers began to reappear. Jennifer and Steve came up tandem, and later Steve told me he had to do a bit of exhaustive encouragement (cursing? threatening?) to get her up and out. She was a pooped puppy.

I rarely have memories of the return from these trips, and this one was no exception. As is usually the case for journeys, it's always a relief to get home.

Commentary on photos:

The two photos of my daughter Jennifer were taken at other times, but serve to show some of the equipment used, as well as before and after a rappel. Note the difference in the facial expressions for each situation. That pretty much says it all.

Cavernos, Cascadas, e Los Federales

On all the excursions we made into the so-called wild, we planned to cram as much into it as time and opportunity allowed. As on all trips, we relied on information from fellow bushwackers to know what places to visit and how to get there. I wasn't yet a seasoned traveler and had some insecurity about every trip. On this trip, taken as usual over Christmas holidays, Steve Olson, Kay Stewart, and Brian Dollar were my traveling companions, and we were relying on Brian's information and guidance. (Recall my previous stories of Brian and his adventures, Ho, Ho, Ho.)

So we made our way in country, camping along way-sides or near springs. Mornings were cool and misty, as was usual for the time of year, and required waking up and making breakfast, coffee being critical. It was on one of these occasions when Steve earned the nickname of Flambo, when he spilled some white gas onto the up-ended five gallon bucket he was using for a table, and set the whole thing on fire. We all had a great laugh except Steve. We also had some good eats at the small cafes along the way, including an open-air *pescaderos* cafe, where I had my first encounter with octopus. When you don't read the language you sometimes get a surprise. It actually wasn't too bad, but the vision of all those little suction cup 'eyes' still haunts me.

I personally did very little caving on this trip. Checking out the countryside, plants and animals and people watching are my favorite entertainments, and I prefer being the support member of the team. We visited a couple of small caves, more realistically described as grottoes, open to the air and requiring only some easy rappelling. To reach one of the caves we hitched a ride on one of the small hand-operated rail cars used by workers to travel between work sites. They were much amused by our poor attempts to communicate in Spanish, but tolerant, and delivered us to our destination.

One cave we looked for was also a shrine to one of the many saints to which people traveled as a pilgrimage, bringing simple offerings of flowers, food, or other gifts. As we left, a pilgrim, poorly dressed in homespun clothing and sandals but gently friendly, offered to share with us the remainder of the food he had brought for his meal and as a gift at the shrine. Wrapped in plantain leaf was a corn tortilla containing lentils, pork, greens and a sauce. Steve and Brian, who were showing the first symptoms of some flu or gut problems, were reluctant to accept, but I was embarrassed to refuse the simple offering, and curious to try something new. He would accept no payment and my *muchos gracias* seemed to please him. I proceeded to devour the most delicious example of indigenous food I have had before or since. Too bad, guys, you have no idea what you missed. And I had no complaints from my g.i. tract either.

Another destination on this trip was a scenic waterfall called Cascada de Tamul. We spent about an hour driving down a rutted dirt road to reach the headwater of the falls. To get to the falls we followed a path walking on mossy mounds of travertine between which flowed the stream that fed it. Looking upstream from the top, we could see some kayakers working their way toward the falls, through which they would have to pass on their way downstream.

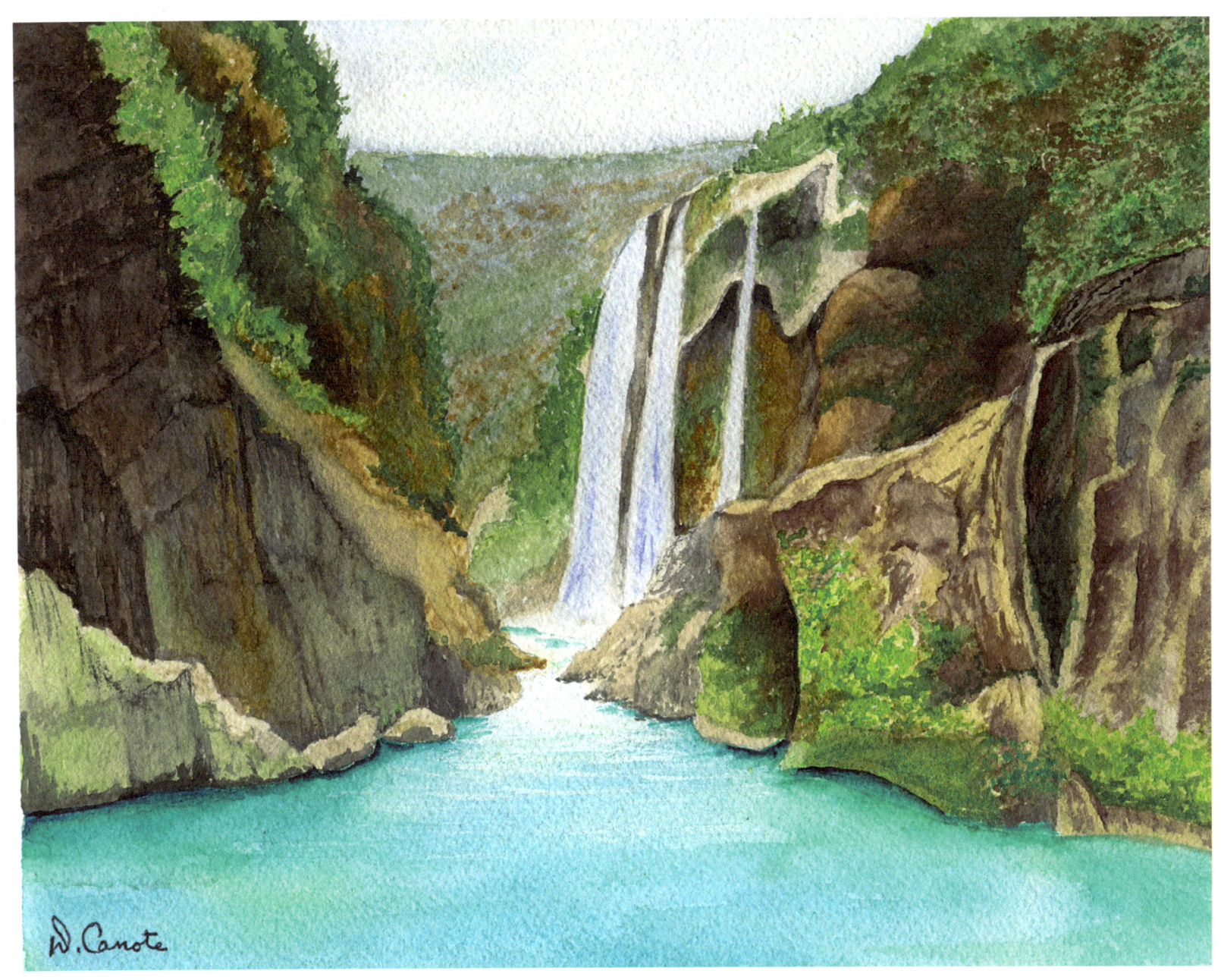

The others decided to work their way to the bottom and get acquainted, while I opted to stay at the top and take a little dip in the pools there. I was feeling a bit brave and, not wanting to get all my clothes soaked, I stripped off and slipped into the clear, cold water. Felt great! Until I heard some voices and here came a group of hikers also out to enjoy the view. What to do? Get out and bare all getting dressed, or stay submerged? Well, I decided to grin and bare it, ha ha. I guess they thought it was no big deal, as we all said "Hi" and they went on. That taught me that even when you think you are out in the middle of nowhere, you aren't.

The next day we met up with some other cavers at a cave that was accessed through a crevice in an otherwise flat pasture. Kay, Brian, and I held down the fort while Steve got his figurative butt kicked by a narrow but deep cave with multiple drops requiring much rigging, wriggling, and otherwise tough conditions. As with many of these trips, Henry Gilsdorf and some of his colleagues brought the rope and led the descent, and he was a hard act to keep up with.

There was one more event on the trip that was memorable but pretty scary. In those years our trips across the border were not too difficult with respect to law enforcement. Most of the drug runners tended to hang out in the western range of the Sierra Madres (Occidentalis), bringing up the illegal stuff from the Baranca del Cobre (Copper Canyon), but one problem the police faced was the smuggling of electronics, although I don't recall whether it was into or out of Mexico. So for whatever reason, it was not uncommon for tourists to be stopped and inspected by the Federales.

We were on our way back north to the border when we came upon a roadblock out in the middle of nowhere. When we stopped, we were met by a group of three or four young men in black teeshirts and camo pants with automatic rifles. Holy simoly! We were asked to exit the vehicle and produce identification for ourselves and the (my!) truck. Being aware of the needed documentation beforehand, I had placed all the vehicle info and such into a manila file folder, which *Steve* packed *where*?

I think he was a bit on edge himself as we tore through the cab, camper, our duffles, etc. looking for it. At one point I asked *el jefe* what would happen if we couldn't find it and he implied that we wouldn't be going anywhere until we did. Steve finally found the little stinker stuffed behind the seat of the cab, where it had slid to the bottom and hidden. Whew!

Then we had another round of anxiety as they asked us to remove all our stuff from the camper to be inspected. Well, we did look pretty disreputable after a week of camping and bouncing around the countryside, fording rivers in my truck with its old, beat-up camper shell with its jerry-rigged canoe racks. Thankfully we had no electronics—radios, TVs, or anything electrical other than battery-powered lights. So we had to load all our gear back up, and let me tell you we didn't waste any time about it. But that wasn't the end of it.

As we were standing around, several of the troup were pointing at my britches and muttering something like, "...*infractione ... infractione*..." Au, oh. It wasn't uncommon for outdoor enthusiasts in the States to wear camos, as they're rugged and comfortable, so of course I had to have a pair on. We were informed that in Mexico they were reserved for the military and it was illegal for civilians to wear them. I gave their leader my most solemn, respectful, deer-in-the-headlights, wet-your-pants look and said, "I'll take them off the first chance I get!" And I did, because who wants to get put in a Mexican jail over a stinking pair of pants!

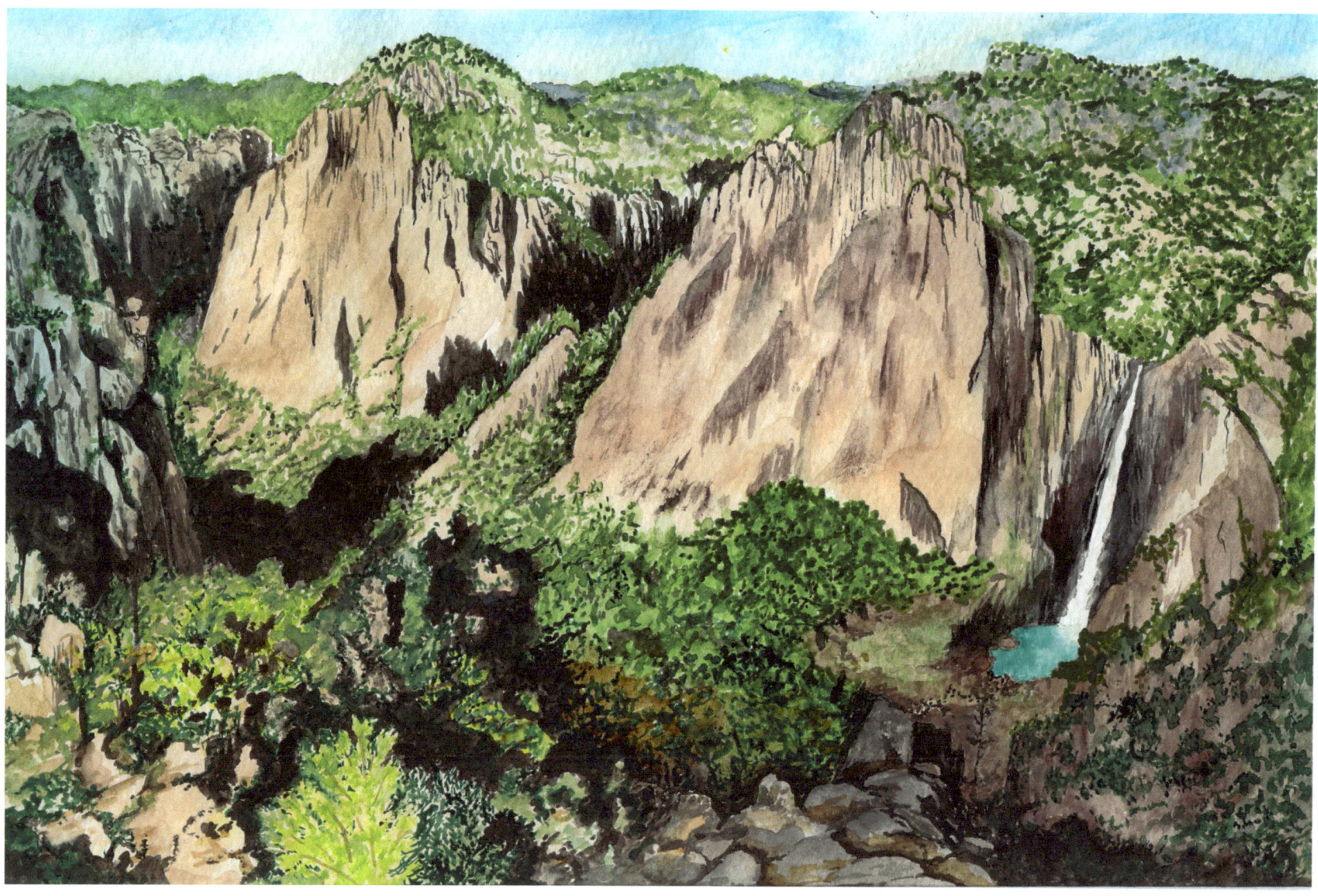

Into the Western Sierra Madres

On the Road to the Baranca del Cobre

Somehow I always thought I would go back, but at this point in my life it looks unlikely. Still, I have some very interesting memories of that last trip. In about 1991, Steve Olson and I made plans for a trip into Mexico's western mountains, the Sierra Madre Occidentales, to see if we could find the Barancha del Cobre, otherwise known as Copper Canyon. Well, rather we would see if we could find our way *to* it, since it is bigger than the Grand Canyon of the Colorado, so it would be pretty hard to miss.

Steve picked me up in Austin, Texas, where I had gone ahead to spend Christmas with family. The day before he got there I came down with the flu—fever and aches, but with no g.i. upset, fortunately. When he got there I was of a mixed frame of mind, but, having made extensive plans and packing all that gear, plus the fact that we were already half way there, off we went, flu and all.

Crossing the border was no big deal in those days, especially out in the area of the Chihuahuan Desert. There really isn't much out there. In fact, as we traveled south the thing that struck me was the absolute lack of light, make that lights, since there were no electric lines into the area. No dusk-to-dawn lights, no porch lights, no houses with windows ablaze. Any light we saw as we drove was a tiny faint glow from candles or lanterns in small houses near the road. The stars were incandescent in the night sky and looked twice as big as they did at home.

Details of our travel are vague, probably due to the fact that I slept in a feverish haze through much of it. The second day in country, we passed through Cuidad, Chihuahua, where we did a little sight seeing. The murals on the wall of the Government Palace were an impressive testament to the history of the city, but even more memorable to me was the 1919 black Dodge touring car in which Pancho Villa was riding when he was assassinated in July of 1923 in the city of Parral. The car was riddled with more than forty bullet holes of large caliber, and Villa was killed instantly. It sits in front of the Historical Museum of the Mexican Revolution and I was viscerally impacted by a part of history that I had only read about or seen in cinema.

As we moved south on our drive, we went deeper and deeper into the Mexican landscape, about one hundred miles west of Cuidad Chihuahua, in search of a reportedly very impressive waterfall called Basaseachic Falls. Let me just say at this point that it takes perseverance and quite a lot of gas to get to anywhere in Mexico. At that time unleaded gas was not readily available in other that the larger cities there, so we had to watch the gauges, plan, and take every opportunity to fill up when we saw an unleaded pump. And also, public restrooms were not common, rest stops generally being anywhere there is enough vegetation to hide behind.

Basaseachic Falls is created by the convergence of two tributary streams which dry up in the spring and autumn, so we were fortunate to see it at its full flow. The streams, which arise in the high mountains, combine to produce the falls which plunge off 807 feet into a pool at the bottom. My painting was done from a montage of half a dozen photos taken from the south overlook and pieced together into a panorama. It brings into perspective the magnitude and severity of the relief in these mountains.

One other memory of this site is noteworthy. We had driven for what seemed like hours over two-lane blacktop road to get to the falls, and finally pulled into a tourist info cabin at the head of the falls. We picked up some information and were ready to do some exploring when we saw another vehicle arrive. Several folks got out and we could hear them conversing in English, so we wandered nearer to see if we could make their acquaintance. As is turned out, the two families were a Mexican couple and an American couple whose daughters were involved in a student exchange program, and the United States couple was from Mexico, Missouri! It just goes to show that no matter how far away from home you get, you can't escape your neighbors.

Not Quite to the Copper Canyon

Before we left for the trip, several experienced Mexico travelers advised us not to go into the mountains without at least *two* spare tires. And of course they were right. We left Basaseachic Falls, made the long drive back to a main highway, and headed south to the town of Creel. This little town of several thousand souls is in the heart of the Sierra Tarahumara, and was at that time considered the gateway to the Copper Canyon area. This region of the Sierra Madre Occidental is home to the indigenous Tarahumara Indians, who refer to themselves as Rarámuri. Creel was originally a logging town, but at this time much of the native timber had been stripped from the region.

As we drove south out of Creel, we saw a man hitchhiking in the same direction. He appeared to be other than native and was dressed in a manner that suggested he might be a safe pick up, so we did. He spoke fluent English and as we visited with him we learned something of his history. His parents came to Mexico originally from Spain. After raising a family, they returned to Spain but he and his sister remained in Mexico.

The gentleman, Francisco Cardenal, was returning to his house, a little off the beaten path, so to speak, and would be grateful for a ride there. We left the main road and inched our way slowly and carefully along a dubious path through boulders and ditches until we came to his little cabin. His vocation was the study of the medicinal plants used by the Rarámuri, about which he had written a book. His native friends had helped him to build his cabin using simple tools (saw and hammer) and lumber hauled, undoubtedly by donkey, from the nearby hills. The hard-packed dirt floor was typical of many of the rural homes we had seen on previous trips to the country, and his furniture was rustic and of the same local lumber, but beautifully made and functional for his purposes. On the wall were shelves of books, and speakers for a battery operated cassette player with an impressive collection of music tapes.

Francisco was a delightful host, modest and willing to speak at length of his studies and experiences. We spent the afternoon and decided to camp there overnight. Being only a one-bedroom house (the loft), there no room in the inn, so there was no option but to sleep in the truck camper. Let me just say that January in those mountains is co-o-old and there is no insulation in the bed of a pickup. The drinking water in our jugs froze and I thought I would too.

The next morning we were preparing to head south when we discovered a tire with a tear in the sidewall. A discussion ensued as to the wisdom of driving further into the mountains with no spare. For me it was a no-brainer: no way, no how. Wisdom prevailed and we headed back north to find a service station that could repair the tire. However, that put the proverbial kibosh on our plans to visit the Copper Canyon. We stopped off in Creel where I bought a copy of Francisco's book, which I still have. I would really like to know more about the native plants he studied and their curative properties, but the book is in Spanish, and I am still looking for a translator.

If you are interested in the area we visited, I highly recommend Jeff Biggers' book, *In the Sierra Madre*, which relates his year-long stay there and gives a highly readable account of the area's people, history, and way of life.

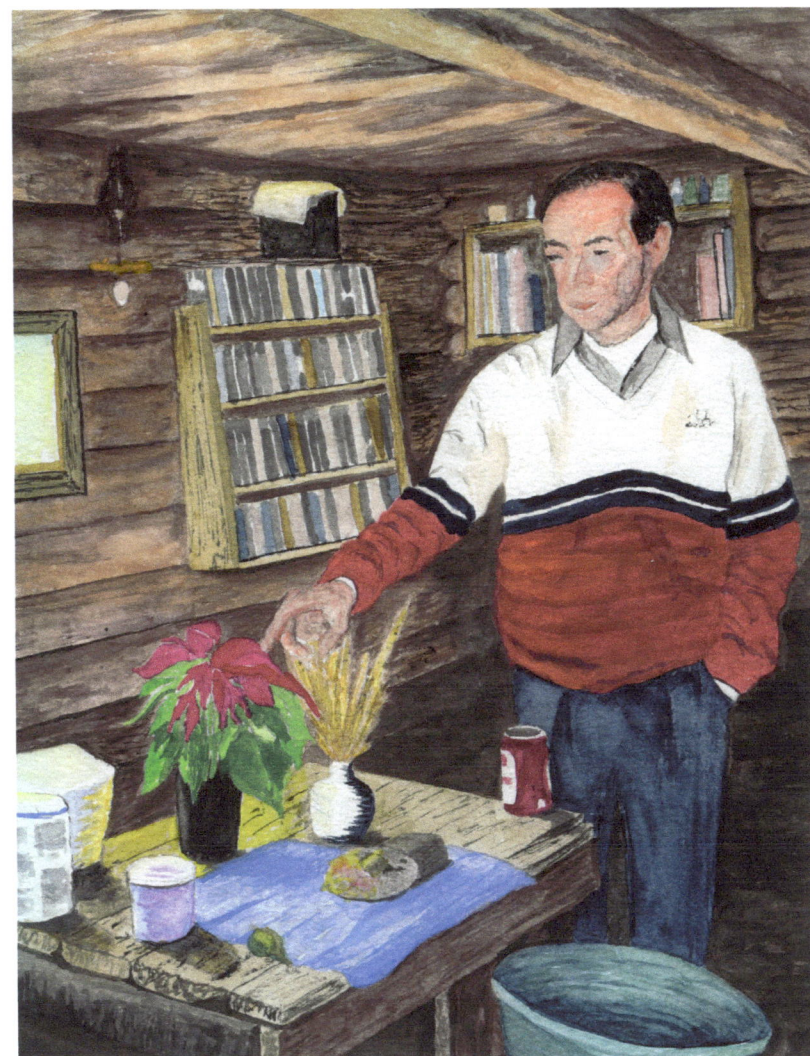

About the Author

Dorothy Canote grew up in Avalon, Missouri, and received her Bachelor of Science in Biology from Missouri Valley College. She earned a Masters degree in Agronomy from the University of Missouri–Columbia, followed by post-graduate studies in Fisheries and Wildlife. Her resume includes eight years as a study director in aquatic toxicology at ABC Labs, finishing her professional career as a science instructor for ten years at Hickman High School in Columbia.

Retirement from teaching was followed by growing produce, herbs, and flowers for the Columbia Farmers Market, during which time she also rediscovered her love for art and turned her hand to watercolor painting. This is Dorothy's second book featuring some of her watercolor paintings and essays about them and the thoughts and experiences they illustrate.

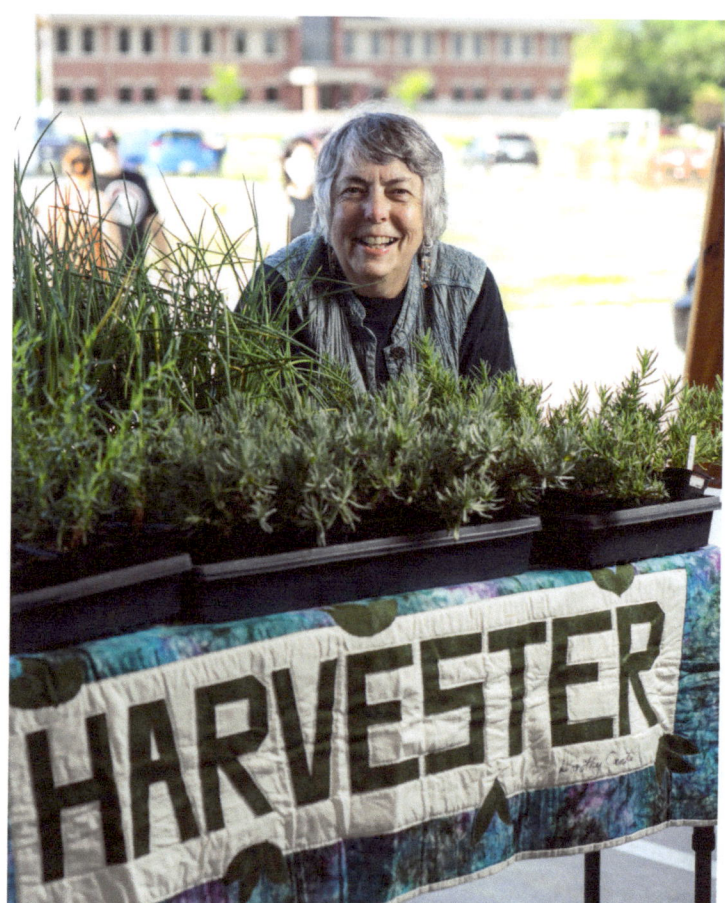